DATE DUE

BIOGRAPHY AND THE HUMAN HEART

HORACE WALPOLE, EARL OF ORFORD

BIOGRAPHY
and the
HUMAN HEART

BY
GAMALIEL BRADFORD

WITH ILLUSTRATIONS

Essay Index Reprint Series

 BOOKS FOR LIBRARIES PRESS
FREEPORT, NEW YORK

STANDARD BOOK NUMBER:
8369-1023-0

LIBRARY OF CONGRESS CATALOG CARD NUMBER:
68-58772

PRINTED IN THE UNITED STATES OF AMERICA

In the world men must be dealt with according to what they are, and not to what they ought to be; and the great art of life is to find out what they are, and act with them accordingly.

CHARLES C. F. GREVILLE

CONTENTS

ILLUSTRATIONS

I
BIOGRAPHY AND THE HUMAN HEART

I

BIOGRAPHY AND THE HUMAN HEART

I

WE LIVE and move in a world of shadows, in which there is one intense reality, the reality called you or I, which perhaps is the vaguest shadow of all. The constant, unfailing, undying effort of our existence is to escape from the hampering prison of the I, and somehow, somewhere, to come into contact with these other shadow lives, which we dimly divine, but never really touch. This passionate desire is the basis of all social activity, and leads us to waste rich hours in dull talk and aimless diversion. It is the basis of all our affections. It is the basis of the alluring, perplexing, tragical, comical mystery of love. The same eternal desire is the basis of our interest in biography. And with this overwhelming instinct in us, it is not strange that we should find an absorbing pleasure in the story of shadow lives, even though poorly written and commonplace.

Moreover, though we live in a shadowy world, the shadows throng and crowd about us and jostle us at every step, with a persistent, inevitable pressure, which we cannot elude or escape. We must adapt and adjust our own action, our conduct, our lives, to theirs, in some fashion, and in order to effect such adjustment, we must give the closest study, conscious or instinctive, from infancy to

3

age, to the nature of these shadows, to their movement and working, to what we assume to be their passions and motives and characters, based on what we conjecture of their similarity to our own. As Greville puts it, in the sentence which I have chosen as an epigraph for this book, 'In the world men must be dealt with according to what they are, and not to what they ought to be; and the great art of life is to find out what they are, and act with them accordingly.'

Thus we have two substantial instincts to account for the universal interest in biography. First, there is the desire to get out of ourselves and into the lives of others. Second, there is the desire and the necessity of understanding others' lives and characters, for the practical purpose of shaping our own by such knowledge. And it is true that neither of these desires can ever be satisfied. We can never in this world escape from the hampering limit of ourselves or really enter into the life of anyone else, however much we may desire to do so. And our knowledge of the lives of others must ever remain shadowy, disappointing, and incomplete. The final test of such knowledge is the prediction of action. And no study, no research, no intellectual equipment has ever yet enabled any one man to foretell with any certainty the action of any other. So that the wisest are often ready to echo the despairing cry of Henry Adams: 'All that Adams ever saw in man was a reflection of his own ignorance.' Yet it is charmingly characteristic of human nature that the very impossibility of satisfying these desires makes them more ardent and more enduring, and we go out of life with the same passionate eagerness to enter into the lives of others and to understand them, that we brought into it.

It is obvious that biography generally deals with the lives of great and prominent individuals. Sir Sidney Lee, the late William R. Thayer, and many others who have written on the subject, tell us that the origin of biography is the desire to commemorate distinguished and worthy persons and to erect an enduring monument of their greatness. No doubt there is a certain truth in this. At the same time I question whether the many who read biography are chiefly moved by the reverent disposition to pay tribute to departed glory. It is true that we are interested to read about the great, who have achieved prominence and success, because we are interested to see wherein we resemble or may resemble them. But I think there is one very practical reason for writing about notable lives: the material for an ample and exhaustive study of such lives, in all phases and all aspects, is abundantly available, whereas for the study of common persons, like you and me, it is not. Yet, if the deeper explanations given above for the passionate interest in biography, the desire to get out of ourselves, and the need of knowing others, are valid, they would apply just as much, and even more, to the study of common lives, of lives of just the quality of yours and mine, as to the lives of those whose fate or genius has set them apart from the generality of men. 'The art of the biographer,' says M. Marcel Schwob, in his too brief essay on the subject, 'should consist in giving as much value to the life of a poor actor as to the life of Shakespeare.' This, of course, requires distinction and modification. At the same time, the life of a shop-girl or a motor-man might be as profoundly interesting as that of a saint or a hero, might even prove to be that of a saint or a hero, if we could get at it. But the shadow life of the shop-girl drifts away in shadow, and the life of the saint is passed in a splendor of limelight which appears to dissipate the shadows, though often it only makes them deeper.

The truth of this contention about the value of common lives appears in the work of the creative artist, whose effort is to give the immortality of beauty to just such common creatures as you and me. Œdipus and Hamlet and Lear, and Juliet and Portia, are not saints and heroes; they are just men and women, as you and I are, and their eternal biographies give the record of simple life with all its torture and all its illusion, just as you and I have to live it, or might have to live it every day.

As ordinary people are the most interesting, even supposing there are any others, so there is value, and perhaps often the greatest value, for biography, in ordinary incidents and experiences. The great crises of life have their immense and lasting importance; but they occur rarely, to many persons they do not occur at all, and when they do occur, it

6

BIOGRAPHY AND THE HUMAN HEART

is in such a turmoil of confusion and unusual circumstance that it is extremely difficult to interpret them. True human value, real insight into life and character, are often given by little things and apparently trivial happenings. A word spoken carelessly, a brief look or gesture, will sometimes tell us more of the history of a soul than elaborate pages of psychological analysis, and persons who are not at all trained in such analysis may interpret the word or the gesture with unerring skill.

Evidently there is distinction needed here, and precisely in this distinction lies the finest art of the biographer. 'It is detail that makes things live,' says Sainte-Beuve. But also, as we all know, there is nothing like detail to kill things. It is all a question of choice. The biographer must not overwhelm us with formless, irrelevant, inconsequent gossip. He must know how to go right straight at the pregnant touch which reveals, to pick that out, to stress it, without over-stressing it, and to leave entirely aside the mass of the insignificant, which merely confuses and obscures. For example, in the elaborate accounts of the death of Daniel Webster, he will pass over much that is merely rhetorical, and will seize and fix at once the tremendous, dramatic incident when the great statesman, after having made a parting profession to his assembled friends and family, sinks back exhausted, and then, recovering, murmurs, 'Have I — wife, children, physicians, friends — have I, on this occasion, said anything unworthy of Daniel Webster?' It is rare that a man sums up his whole life and character so completely in a phrase. These are the common human touches that we look for; and when we get them, we feel, as Sainte-Beuve puts it, that the veil is torn away, and we read bare soul.

II

Having thus established the infinite identity in infinite isolation of the common human heart, it becomes worth while to follow the varied phases of that identity, the intimate fibres, by the throbbing of which in our hearts common creatures like you and me are able to understand the biographies of great and little and to enter with passionate interest into the doings and the sufferings of Cæsar and Napoleon, of Joan of Arc and Mary Stuart, as of Mr. and Mrs. Jones just around the corner. It is these fundamental common human elements that make biography real, that make it possible, that make the story of one over and over again the story of all.

Take first love, the basic instinct of sex, perhaps the most universal and the most easily understood of all human passions and motives, not only in its grosser foundation, but in its subtle, infinitely varied and complicated refinements. Love in its more serene and normal course, if it ever has such, love in its robust, wholesome, insignificant domesticity, is not perhaps largely developed in biographies, though the wise know how to recognize and to appreciate its value. But love as an abnormal manifestation, love in its ardor, its unrest, its infinite renewal, its endless disappointment, and satiety, and despair, the tragic complication of these appears over and over in biography, as we most of us know something of it at one time or another in our own lives.

Sine dolore non vivitur in amore, says the simple, profound author of the *Imitation*: there is no love without suffering, either love human or love divine. So we get poignant tragedy like that of Keats, in which love and death and glory are so deeply intertwined that they make an inextricable tangle of supreme despair. And again, the lighter, wayward follies of the male sex may not seem to have much suffering about them, and we find the record of the vagaries of a Pepys or a Casanova. But the lining of such vagaries means suffering in the end, for someone, and the last volume of Pepys's *Diary* is a naked, tragic record of agony that the vagaries brought to him.

With women it seems as if the suffering were more intense and more constant. Even in the secure serenity of settled matrimonial peace, something of longing, of vague discontent, of desire unrealized, is apt to creep in, and a million women will understand the cry of Sarah Butler, writing to her absent husband, who was too busy for sentimental cares: 'Oh, dearest, I feel just as Benny does, when he creeps into my lap at night and wants me to rock and sing to him. And there is nobody to rock or sing or care anything about me....

BIOGRAPHY AND THE HUMAN HEART

Do you lay down my letters after you read them with a doubtful, unpleasant feeling, or do you, *hum — ah — hm*, or do you say, ah, well, a good many words about nothing? Or have you other letters of greater interest? Are mine hastily scanned and thrown down? ... I especially wish tonight that somebody loved me, a little, I am so tired; but I hardly think there is anyone can, it is so much work.' Or we may have the distilled essence of passion in the letters of Mademoiselle de L'Espinasse: 'I do nothing but love, I know nothing but love.' Or again, we have the large Odyssey of George Sand, seeking, questing, trying, with inexhaustible ardor, reading remote, profound, and subtle secrets into the cruder processes and purposes of nature, compelling the love of man into the imperishable love of God, determined not to recognize a simple orgy of the senses in a mysterious spiritual communion, in the brutal phrase of the poet,

> Fond maids, who love with mind's fine stuff, would mend
> Which Nature purposely of bodies wrought.

But widely and diversely as the story may be written, there is always something in it that comes home to all of us.

As love is a universal element of biography, so, in almost equal measure, is ambition, the desire for success and glory, to do something notable in the world that men will cherish and remember. To be sure, in most of us this desire dies out and is forgotten in the pressure of petty daily needs and the growing sense that it will never be realized. But most of us have known it at one time or another, most of us have at least dreamed of greatness, of doing and achieving things that will be remembered and are worthy to be so. We have all known enough of the sense of power, of the luxury of controlling and dominating the fortunes of others, or at any rate of wishing to do so, to understand what Voltaire means when he says, 'I love passionately to be master.' We have all dreamed the dream of glory sufficiently to enter into the cry of Frederick the Great: 'Glory... is folly, but it is folly that you cannot shake off, when once you get it fastened upon you.' Or there is the ambition of the artist, the undying desire to create things beautiful and to be forever honored for such creation. The poet or the painter toils for years in silence at the masterpiece which is to bring him undying fame. The more immediate artist, the actor or the singer or the preacher — or, if you like, the athlete, since those supreme artists, the Greeks, thought him an artist too — snatches the brief fruition of glory in the maddening applause of the moment, which flares out and is forgotten. And it is delightful to hear the gluttons of glory so often proclaim their indifference to it. Cicero, to whom it was the breath of life, cries out, 'If there was ever anyone, by nature and reason and reflection, indifferent to empty praise and the chatter of the vulgar, it is I.' So, many other statesmen and many other artists. Yet in more genuine moments the real nature underneath is manifest enough. Daniel Webster, on a calm moonlight night, confides to his friend that ambition is the essence of his soul. Charlotte Cushman, when she returns to the stage, after a prolonged absence, and once more warms to the enthusiasm of thousands, throws up her hands to heaven, and cries in ecstasy, 'Oh, how have I lived all these years without this?'

And the common man and woman — that is, you and I — sighs or smiles, and remarks that he has lived very well all these years without anything of the kind, and that all this business of biographies of glory is very far away from him, as from Cicero. But when you think a minute, you see that ambition is nothing but the hunger for success, and that there is no great or little to that hunger, which is simply the absorbing interest of our lives. The common man may want a local honor in the little village where he lives, the presidency of a petty board or club, and the effort to get it may cost him as much life — and character — as the empire cost Napoleon. Or he may seek success in business, to outdo a competitor, to reach a certain goal of fortune, to own a pretty little house that he has long coveted, and the ambition for these things becomes as mad and as engrossing as Charlotte Cushman's desire to see thousands at her feet. Even our diversions get their zest from the same passion to excel and to surpass. A woman wants the leadership of her little social circle, and destroys her health and wastes her money to get it. A man catches the golf fever, and the peace of home, the quiet of easy days, even the necessary attention to make his business go as it should, are all forgotten in the determination that Smith and Jones shall not carry away the prize. So ambition, in one form or another, puts us all on a level with kings and saints, and it happens that their biographies might very often be our own.

Or, again, another huge element of this universal story of humanity, which is your story and mine, is the element of money, from which high and low, good and bad, never altogether escape. 'When it is a question of money, everybody is of the same religion,' says Voltaire. There are few biographies which do not deal with this matter more or less, and few that do not give valuable light on the various problems connected with it. Read the *Diary* of Pepys for thrift and happy results of conscientious care without undue parsimony. Read the equally illuminating *Diary* of Haydon for the unfortunate working of opposite tendencies, as in the ghastly veracity of the following: 'The evening passed on, as it always does in a family where the father has no money. The children smoke it, the servants suspect it. There is either an over-kindness, an over-irritability, or an affected unconcern, which opens the lynx eyes.'

There is the hideous slowness and burdensome self-denial with which money is accumulated. There is the difficulty of holding on to it, when accumulated, as expressed in the words of one of wide experience in such matters: 'We see ten men who can get money for one who can keep it.' There is the appalling and disastrous and unaccountable facility with which money slips away. And we have the comment on the whole matter, in the biography of the author of the *Elegy in a Country Churchyard*, a comment which deserves to become classic and to be known to everyone for its depth and breadth of energetic truth: 'Swift says somewhere that money is liberty, and I fear money is friendship, too, and society and almost every external blessing. It is a great, though ill-natured, comfort to see most of those who have it in plenty without pleasure, without liberty, and without friends.'

III

As biography is woven largely out of these vast common impulses and motives and passions and needs, so there enter into it the general human weaknesses and frailties and defects. The little secret flaws and faults, which we all endeavor to cover and believe peculiar to ourselves, may often be discerned and traced in the stories of the great ones of the earth, and it cannot be denied that such tracing brings a certain caressing comfort with it.

Thus, as there is ambition, and success, there is inevitably failure, and in all human life, the greatest as well as the least, the two go hand in hand, if indeed the failure does not bear immeasurably the greater proportion of the two. It is not only those who appear to have lost the prizes, but those who appear to have got them, who register their fail-

ures, and taste all the bitterness of disappointment.
If you are Napoleon, you go from victory to victory, you pile Jena upon Marengo, and Wagram
upon Austerlitz, and you set an imperial crown on
top of it all, and then you bury yourself in the
calamities of Spain and Russia, and the horror of
Waterloo seems greater than the glory of any
triumph.

If you are an artist, you write a play or paint a
picture that takes the attention of the world. The
critics flatter you, the dealers follow you, money
pours in upon you, you think you are the equal of
Shakespeare and Phidias, your exaltation knows no
bounds. Perhaps the reception of the very next
work is different. The critics are critical. The public turns to something else. Even at the best, you
grow older, if you have the misfortune to live, and
to see your work and your name forgotten is worse
than never to have had them known. Also, the
nameless, causeless, inexplicable depression and
discouragement, which haunt you and me, which
we are ashamed of yet cannot conquer, are just as
familiar to the great and the successful, and may be
read at large in their biographies, for our consolation and encouragement. We have it in Gray, the
author of the best-loved poem in the English language: 'I seem to myself to inspire everything
around me with *ennui* and dejection.' We read of
Alphonse Daudet saying, when he was at the height
of popularity and success: 'My afternoons are forlorn beyond expression: there are times when I wish

I could cry like a woman.' And in the field of public life we have John Quincy Adams, after he had reached the climax of American ambition in being President, writing: 'My whole life has been a succession of disappointments. I can scarcely recollect an instance of success to anything that I ever undertook.' And surely a man who had never been president of anything could not breathe a more melancholy sigh of failure.

These dark fits of depression are, of course, closely connected with physical weakness, and the biography of great and little is filled with the record of such weakness, and it has an absorbing interest, simply because you and I, no matter who we are, sooner or later are bound to have such weakness to contend with, in ourselves and in those we love.

There is the wonder of robust health, and the close relation of it to great achievement, and we read of men who can dispense with food and sleep, till we think that we, too, might accomplish anything if we were like them. Goethe was a great lover and a great artist, but he had the physique of a Greek Apollo to help him. Napoleon could get along indefinitely with four hours' sleep. Who could not win battles with twenty hours out of the twenty-four to think about them? Edison, again, tells us that four hours' sleep is enough for any man, and the triumphs of his laboratory bear witness to the results of such physical power. But those who have health are apt to abuse it. Napoleon won an empire by going without sleep, but when it came to

Waterloo, he had to pay the penalty, and we read that during that battle the lack of sleep made him a very different man from what he had been. Scott poured out novel after novel, written while other men were sleeping, but his brain failed him before his body did, exhausted with excessive activity and over-strain. Perhaps a little less achievement goes with longer life, after all.

And biographical records are filled with the detail of sickness and physical decay. Diarists and letter-writers may omit to mention the welfare of their souls; they rarely overlook the weakness and affliction of their bodies. But what is chiefly of profit for most of us is the story of those who have done great things, in spite of physical weakness and limitation. It is Lanier or Keats, writing supreme poetry when the hand of death is upon him. The mortal touch may affect the quality of the work, for better, for worse; but what impresses us is the persistent courage which battles to the end against decay and despair. Or, still more, it is Darwin, all whose later years were one long disease, whose working hours were cut almost, and sometimes quite, to nothing, yet who toiled with unconquerable pertinacity to give the world a theory that changed the whole constitution of thought, and did it without complaint and without petulance to the end.

Besides physical health, there is moral health, or ill-health, which makes the stuff and matter of biography, because it makes the stuff and matter of all life. There is moral health as regards one's self, in the aspect of temptation and yielding. Some of the amplest of biographical records, like the *Confessions* of Saint Augustine, deal fully with human nature in this aspect, too fully, some of us think, with amplification of sin, for the sake of emphasizing repentance. There is the temptation of drink, as we find it minutely and curiously exposed in the narrative of John B. Gough. There are the manifold liabilities of sex, exhibited only too freely in records of every kind. There is sex, joyous, naked, and unashamed, as we find it in Casanova or in the wild *Diary* of Aaron Burr. There is sex, timid, respectable, cautious, repentant, as we find it in the *Diary* of Pepys. There are the temptations of money, mere disorder and incompetence, as they are depicted so tragically in the *Diary* of Haydon, sordid and petty as they appear in Augustine or Rousseau, on a larger and more dubious scale, as we meet them in the lives of men like Blaine or Ben Butler. And again, there is the inner spiritual weakness, the mere infirmity of will eaten away by the excessive power or subtlety of the pure intelligence, as it is analyzed in the strange histories of Amiel or Barbellion.

Further, there is moral defect or ill-health in the vastly more important forms that affect others. There is good, honest, straight-out hate, and it seems as if this were now not quite the force in the world that it has sometimes been, as if men, by acquiring a little broader knowledge of life, were coming to see the folly of mere blind, useless animosity. Yet perhaps the decay of loving goes with the decay of hating, if there really is such. Dr. Johnson loved a good hater: it seems to me that I hardly know one. Certainly the furious hatreds of a man like Benvenuto Cellini would seem to have been more common in the Renaissance than they are now, at any rate with their violent and puerile excesses.

But if there is less open hate, there is still plenty of covert meanness and jealousy and spite, left in the world, and always will be, so long as men are convinced that they fail and others get ahead because of lucky accidents and unfair advantages. Sometimes the meaner motives are acutely conscious of themselves, and those who cherish them recognize them, even while they indulge them still. Yet how rare is it, in biography, to find such complete frankness as Heine's, when he says of the attacks upon Goethe and the motive of them: 'I know this motive exactly in the case of only one person, and as I am myself this person, I can confess it honestly: it was envy.'

But though we overlook these passions in ourselves, and conceal and obscure them with every possible excuse, we are, alas, only too ready to attribute them to others, and to assume that they base their conduct on motives which we should instantly reject as the origin of our own. Nothing can be more instructive than to watch this tendency at work in a man so high-minded, so conscientious, and so critical of himself as John Quincy Adams, and his huge diary is a remarkable exposure of his own temper in bitter and cruel analysis of the lives and characters of those about him, as when he complains of 'the rotten heart of Daniel Webster.' Now Webster's heart was no more rotten than Adams's was: it was just human, that was all.

At the bottom of all these more remote and indirect developments lie the bare, fundamental impulses and movements of the human heart, and biography exposes these also, remorselessly, for the profit of those who care to read. There is self-preservation, perhaps the root of all, and its correlative of fear. We like to read of magnificent courage, and those who have it least admire it most. We like the natural intrepidity of General Grant, whose stolid nerves did not feel danger, and whose well-poised brain worked as well, or even better, when peril was thickest about him. We like better still the acquired self-possession of General Lee, whose nerves had no such natural stolidity, but who had followed duty till he was perfectly indifferent whether it led him over battle-fields or flower-gardens.

And back of the varied phases of fear, from little tormenting frets and worries to vague distress, is the intense concrete reality of pain and the obscure mystery of death. And biography is as full of death as life is. Some of us face death with a smile, or affect to do so, and some disguise it and veil it with sounding phrases, and most forget it so far as possible. But it has an unpleasant habit of naked and ghastly intrusion at inconvenient moments.

In the greatest biography of the world we read that Dr. Johnson, a sage who had wit, wisdom, and religion to support him, was haunted by the constant dread of death and sought every solace and diversion to keep it at arms' length. In a very different biographical record, the *Journal* of the Goncourts, we find four great French novelists discussing their attitude toward the same universal bugbear and agreeing that it was an obsession of horror that they could hardly escape.

The supreme antidote for this horror has always been the belief in the life after death, and no form of biography is richer and more varied than that of the saints who have been preoccupied with the antidote, have framed their action upon it, and have done their best to impart it to others and to teach others to avail themselves of it. The basis of this belief in the future has always been the belief in a personal God, who had made man for a higher and more enduring destiny than any that he can discover on this earth. As Amiel puts the belief and the passion in its highest intensity: 'There is but one thing necessary: to possess God.... All the senses, all the forces of mind and soul, all exterior resources are but avenues leading to the divine, are but so many means for approaching and adoring God.'

To some of us it appears that this sense of the divine has been much weakened of late by the altered scientific interpretation of the material world. Such weakening may or may not be justified. The point is that it has taken an immense and solid hold not only upon the profane and irreligious, but perhaps even more upon the religious as well. How many thousands of those whose parents were securely and solidly fixed in orthodox belief now find themselves in the position so vividly expressed in one of the most recent of autobiographies, that of Mr. Theodore Dreiser: 'Up to this time there had been in me a blazing and unchecked desire to get on and the feeling that in doing so we did get somewhere; now in its place was the definite conviction that spiritually we got nowhere, that there was no hereafter, that one lived and had his being because one had to, and that it was of no importance. Of one's ideals, struggles, deprivations, sorrows and joys, it could only be said that they were chemic impulses, something which for some inexplicable but unimportant reason responded to and resulted from the hope of pleasure and the fear of pain. Man was a mechanism, undevised and uncreated, and a badly and carelessly driven one at that.'

It seems that this spiritual, or unspiritual, attitude has spread far and dug deep, and one wonders how it will be reflected in the biography of the future. In that of the past, God was an enormous element, and until death can be eliminated also, one cannot help suspecting that He will continue to keep quite a hold upon biography and upon life.

BIOGRAPHY AND THE HUMAN HEART

IV

So far we have been emphasizing human identity as the basis of biography. It is obvious that human difference is also an important and conspicuous element of it, and when one has once established and recognized the identity as a basis, the study of difference becomes almost, if not quite, as interesting as the study of resemblance. Even assuming that the same broad, substantial motives are common to all human beings, that characters are woven together of innumerable strands of identical qualities, these motives and qualities appear in very varying degrees and in surprisingly shifting combinations. In fact, if one merely surveys the surface of biographical research, one is apt to be supremely impressed with the diversity, especially as each individual who discusses himself is naturally disposed to declare, like Rousseau, at the beginning of the *Confessions*: 'I am not made like any of those whom I have seen; I venture to believe that I am not made like any who exists. If I am not better, I am different.' A deeper and more thoughtful investigation may return almost with monotony to the resemblance beneath these differences, but certainly the casual reader of biographical narration thinks first of the astounding variety of careers and of souls. Take, in the extremes, such a figure as Rousseau himself, tossed and beaten and baffled through a long life by tempestuous impulses of uncontrolled emotion and passion, and then turn to John Stuart Mill and the picture in his autobiography of the opposite, of the patient, oppressive, closely dominating control of the guiding intelligence. Take, side by side, and in their correspondence so closely thrown together, two such figures as Thomas Jefferson and John Adams, setting their souls sharply and vividly before us in their long exchange of letters, and souls so different, yet both so human. Or, within the memory of all of us, take Roosevelt and Wilson, alike in some elements of their careers, alike in some movements of their fate and in the vast reach of their ambition, yet so different in the modification of their characters in working toward their ends. And their biographies are full of ample instruction for both difference and identity.

The concrete point of difference that, of course, impresses us most is that of success, since success, great or little, is what we are all looking for and living for. It seems as if the differences between men were the one thing that was important, when we see some, perhaps hardly out of their teens, stepping quietly forward and snatching the prizes of life, getting money, getting glory, getting usefulness, getting applause and laudation everywhere, while others, who feel themselves at any rate to be equally worthy, toil for years and get no prizes at all, nothing but rebuff and discouragement and rejection and disgust.

Yet, when we look more closely, those who do

not win contrive to find their consolations. At least there is consolation in the belief that success is not so much a matter of internal difference as of the unequal gifts of fortune. Men get into great places and do great things in so many instances because the right opening comes at the right time, because the door flies back just as you happen to be passing and ready to step into it. As a wide and keen observer of men has it: 'If I were a great man... when I had gained a hundred battles, I would keep well in the background, sure that, if I did not, you would soon look me over from head to foot and find resemblances to other men, instead of being impressed with the difference.'

To turn to concrete biographical cases. If Napoleon had happened upon a peaceful, secure period of history, would his supreme organizing power and his command of men have done all they did for him? If Cromwell had lived a hundred years earlier or later, would he not have passed away as a humble, humdrum bourgeois, unregarded and forgotten? The talents of Grant were talents of war. They did not get him far in peace, and probably never would have. Robert E. Lee is a more striking instance still. Lee had passed fifty, an esteemed but comparatively undistinguished officer of engineers. His natural modesty and reserve would always have kept him from pushing himself to the front. But the critical necessity of the times pushed him there and made him one of the great heroes of his age, when, if it had not been for opportunity, he would hardly have figured in the world's lasting record at all.

And, as success is largely the product of opportunity, so it appears to be often achieved by spiritual limitations, or even by negative qualities, a reflection amazingly comforting for those who have to do without it. A wide intellectual variety and adaptability sometimes hamper and detract. The man who succeeds is the man of one idea, who is possessed, obsessed by it, who puts aside all other interests of business and pleasure to achieve what he wants. If Darwin had had broader intellectual and æsthetic interests, he might not have observed scientific facts with such intense concentration and might not have hit upon the theory that revolutionized the world.

The same thing appears in practical life. To do things in business or in politics, you do not have to be equipped with modesty, or with sensibility, or with sympathy. A ready tongue and a blithe indifference to the feelings of others go a long way. Take the crucial illustration in American life, the long roll of presidents. It is obvious at once that comparative mediocrity plays a very large place there. To trace the various causes of this would be a study as fascinating as it would be complicated; but it is, at any rate, undeniable that great intellectual ability and depth and force of character, even when driven by unconquerable ambition, do not always arrive, when mediocrity does.

BIOGRAPHY AND THE HUMAN HEART

V

It cannot be too much emphasized that, in urging the human identity as the basis of biography, we are not endeavoring to drag the great down to our level, but instead are seeking to raise ourselves to theirs. Some of us rebel most energetically against the whole position of Carlyle and Nietzsche as to heroes and supermen, against the natural but fatal tendency to exalt a few chosen specimens as wholly apart and different, born and created to trample upon the ordinary, subordinate herd which is composed of you and me. The differences, if you like, the superiorities, of these individuals, are obvious and undeniable, but the more closely one studies human nature, the more one is impressed with the fundamental, essential resemblances, and the cardinal fact, that the same good and evil are latent, if not always patent, in us all. When Rousseau, who posed and is posed as the typical democrat, cries out, in flattery of Frederick the Great and his marshal, Keith, 'These elevated spirits speak among themselves a language which vulgar souls will never understand,' he is misreading and misinterpreting, for in one sense we can never understand each other, and in another there is nothing that we cannot understand, if we know how to look in our own hearts.

It is precisely this deeper instinct of humanity that is at the bottom of the current fashion of what are called destructive, iconoclastic biographies.

BIOGRAPHY AND THE HUMAN HEART

There is the effort to get at the fact of things, to shake the kernel of human truth out of the husk of age-old reputation and glory. And no doubt some good reputations look tattered and shriveled when they have been put through the process, and the kernel of human truth in them shrinks to amazingly little.

No doubt, also, other elements enter in, besides the pure love of common human truth. There is the instinct of smartness and cleverness in the biographer, which, in literature as in life, show themselves too easily in carping and picking flaws. There is the instinct of envy which tears greatness down, simply because it cannot rise itself. And there is the commercial pest, the unfortunate facility in making money out of scandalous assaults upon things that the world has been taught to revere.

Yet, even recognizing and allowing for all these drawbacks, the fashion of critical biography is a thoroughly healthy one, and is not likely soon to pass away. It is founded fundamentally upon the sense of human fellowship. After all, if the great were totally unlike us and belonged to a different world, they would not interest us in the least. We study them, we love them, we follow their careers with absorbed attention, because we see in them the full and rich development of powers and desires that we discern in ourselves, but have allowed to atrophy from lack of nourishment and favoring circumstance. The value of this emphasis of human unity comes precisely in the force of stimulus and example that it brings with it.

And it is here that we see the folly and the failure of the pious, the exemplary biography, which, instead of revealing the subject as human, carefully hides and obscures all those weaknesses and failings which mark him as essentially at one with humanity. As Sir Sidney Lee points out, there are two methods of accomplishing this, the method of suppressing facts and the method of misrepresenting them; but whatever method is adopted, the result for biography is disastrous, and the extent to which it has always prevailed is unbelievable. Even in Plutarch, whose immense, inborn curiosity inclined him to be duly critical, the preaching habit is sometimes too evident. It probably reaches its climax in our own Parson Weems's *Life of Washington*, which should be carefully turned over to be fully appreciated. The spirit in which the work is done and the quality of the workmanship can be fully understood from Weems's account of the means adopted by Washington's father to induce the boy to share presents with his friends: 'To enable him to do this with more alacrity, his father would remind him of the love which he would thereby gain and the frequent presents which would in return be made to him.'

The true, the only possible, value of greatness as an example to littleness, is in showing the little that it may become great, on the basis of a deeper identity between the two. Human greatness is

great only because it is human. The greatness
which cannot bear to have its humanity exposed is
shallow, petty, insignificant, and unenduring. All
men who are really great can afford to be really
human, and to be shown to be so.

VI

From this point of view, of the common human
basis and the human value of biography, its possibilities in education would seem as if they might
perhaps be more utilized than they have been. And
in the present state of educational problems any
clue that offers help should not be disregarded.

Up to a hundred years ago the ideal of a liberal
education was still securely established. A solid
training in the Greek and Latin classics, with a certain amount of mathematics, logic, and philosophy,
was sufficient to provide a basis of culture by which
educated men were able to understand each other
and to communicate in a common language. This
theory of a liberal education has now utterly
vanished. Greek has gone, never to return. Latin
may or may not follow it. In any case, no one can
expect that Cicero and Horace will ever again
supply the foundation of intellectual nourishment
for the mass of cultivated people.

The nineteenth century, in the first triumph of
its acquisition of all sorts of knowledge, especially
scientific, eagerly and happily rushed to complete
the overthrow of this classical ideal, confident that
a more concrete universal mental training would

take the place of it with entire success. That hope was soon disappointed. It became evident that the vast increase of possible information, in all directions, would be beyond the grasp of any human intellect, even to summarize or synthesize. At the first dawning of the new day, Voltaire cried, 'The multitude of books is making us ignorant.' What would he have said of the oppressive, smothering tide of accumulated individual ignorance that was to follow? *The Education of Henry Adams* is the epic narrative of one who lived a vast Odyssey of effort to extract education from this hopelessly accelerating mass, and was driven to the conclusion I have already quoted, 'All that Adams ever saw in man was a reflection of his own ignorance.'

This hopelessness of the abstract mastery of universal knowledge as a substitute for the older liberal education, has forced some of the wisest to fall back upon a merely practical view. Knowing is impossible, doing is all. Teach men to earn their living, to fight their way in the world, to stand upon their own feet, give them 'vocational training' enough, and let them go: you can do no more for them. Taken in its largest sense, that the object of education is not to know, but to live, there is much to be said for this view; but it is, to say the least, susceptible of dangerous and dire perversion.

Now, it seems as if just here the concrete and practical conception of biography might help. And those who know of it are watching with intense curiosity and sympathy the striking effort of Professor Ambrose White Vernon, to build up, at Carleton College, and again at Dartmouth, the first academic department of Biography, in America, if not anywhere. If it can be carried out and developed successfully, this would seem to be one of the most fruitful educational departures that has been attempted for many a year.

After all, the individual human being is the centre of the world, and perhaps no better key can be chosen to help human beings to understand the world. The human being is all of history. He makes it and in turn is made by it. To understand the great movements of history, you cannot have a richer clue than personalities as they intertwine with each other to make events. But the same is true of all other fields of human interest. In literature, in art, in science, in religion, there is always the man, first and last. Get at the man, and you will have double interest in the work. Know the man, or try to know him, and the work will have new significance and far more widely reaching interest.

The educational value of this personal clue is that it appeals to young and old alike. The smallest child takes the human view of things and likes to know what men did, so far as it is within his capacity. And gray age can never be satiated with the variety of problems that can never be solved.

The personal clue is the one above all others that relates the arts and sciences to each other. For, however they may differ in details, the impelling force that drives men to work at them is substantially the same. And by beginning with the human element, you insensibly open out before your pupil all the wide and varying fields of thought. If he has become intensely interested in the men who are working in these fields, he cannot avoid some measure of interest in the fields themselves.

But the supreme value of this educational use of biography is for the conduct of our lives. It teaches us to understand the lives and the motives of others, and nothing is more helpful to us in living our own. To study others, to know others, even in the very moderate degree in which it is possible, helps us to put ourselves in others' places and to put others in ours, and the outcome of such knowledge must necessarily be at least some increase in patience, in sympathy, in tolerance, in love.

In other words, biography is, or should be, or might be, the yeast, the ferment, of the human spirit, which should stir and rouse it to the highest sense of its own achievement and its own powers. Biography affords endless entertainment. But it affords far more than entertainment. It is the record of life, and life is the one supreme thing that interests us all, because we all have to live it.

II
HENRY WADSWORTH LONGFELLOW

CHRONOLOGY

HENRY WADSWORTH LONGFELLOW
Born, Portland, Maine, February 27, 1807.
Graduated from Bowdoin College, 1825.
In Europe, 1826–1829.
Professor at Bowdoin, 1829–1835.
Married Mary Storer Potter, September, 1831.
In Europe, 1835, 1836.
Wife died, 1835.
Professor at Harvard, 1836–1855.
Married Frances Elizabeth Appleton, July 13, 1843.
Evangeline published, 1847.
Hiawatha published, 1855.
Wife died, July, 1861.
Tales of a Wayside Inn published, 1863.
Translation of Dante published, 1867.
Died, Cambridge, March 24, 1882.

HENRY WADSWORTH LONGFELLOW

HENRY WADSWORTH LONGFELLOW

I

BIOGRAPHERS of Longfellow frequently quote the remark of Emerson, when his memory was breaking, but his spiritual insight was as keen as ever. Standing by the coffin of the dead poet, he said, 'That gentleman was a sweet, beautiful soul, but I have entirely forgotten his name.'

The repetition of the eulogy might provoke a petulant reaction against it, if it did not acquire fresh depth and significance with every step we make in the knowledge of Longfellow's life. Two observers, so different from each other and from Emerson as Lowell and Mr. Howells, use language even stronger. Lowell said, in dedicating the Westminster Abbey bust, 'Never was a private character more answerable to public performance than that of Longfellow. Never have I known a more beautiful character.' And Mr. Howells writes: 'As for his goodness, I never saw a fault in him.... All men that I have known, besides, have had some foible,... or some meanness, or pettiness, or bitterness; but Longfellow had none, nor the suggestion of any.'

This is high praise for frail human nature, but the careful study of Longfellow's life and work, in close comparison with a great many other lives and works, goes a long way toward bearing it out.

Let us consider first the qualities more personal to the man himself. His purity of life and thought, from youth up, hardly needs attesting. When he was living alone, as a student in Paris, at the age of nineteen, he writes, 'I am delighted with Paris, where a person if he pleases can keep out of vice as well as elsewhere.'

He did keep out of it, and we need no more than his own word to convince us; for if he was notable for purity, he was notable also for truth. A singular, sweet candor marks all his words about himself, whether reported by others or recorded by his own pen. This sometimes goes so far as an expression of noble confidence in his achievement. For instance, he says of *Hyperion*: 'I look upon the work of my hands with a very complacent smile; and it will take a good deal of persuasion to convince me that the book is not good.' But with all his frankness, such self-satisfaction is rare, because, though he spoke of himself honestly, he spoke seldom. A friend, seeking information and not getting it, urged, 'yet you confessed to me once.' 'No,' interrupted Longfellow, laughing, 'I think I never did.' Even in his intimate letters, even in his diary, where his own affairs are necessarily discussed, absolute and genuine modesty is as marked as candor.

He was eminently modest as to his scholarship, though it was sound and broad. From early youth he was a teacher, but he took on none of the teacher's haunting pedantry and disposition to enlighten the world. He was a good deal more ready to learn from others than to teach them. And though he naturally loved and sought refinement, and even luxury, his manners were perfectly simple because his heart was. It did not come easy to him to mix loudly with his fellows, whether high or humble, and it is said that he 'never got on intimate terms with any but his own set of associates.' But there never was a truer democrat in the deepest essentials of democracy.

It might seem at times as if he lived a life of leisure and even indolence. Yet, if to be proudly busy in achieving things of immense profit and delight to millions is to be active, no man's life was more so. He himself earnestly denies that indolence has any part in things neglected:

> Nor indolence, nor pleasure, nor the fret
> Of restless passions that would not be stilled,
> But sorrow, and a care that almost killed,
> Kept me from what I may accomplish yet.

And when grief threatens to overcome him, his remedy is strenuous labor: 'I find no other way of keeping my nerves quiet than this — namely, to do with all my might whatever I have to do, without thinking of the future, in which most people live.'

Even, under his apparent rich serenity, he has a strong touch of the Puritan, New England conscience, which grows restless in the enjoyment of leisure that is perfectly innocent. 'How lazy the seaside is! If one only had no conscience! But idleness makes me unhappy.' And that cunning, relentless taskmaster, conscience, makes him not only labor, but labor with far-reaching precision and design. He plans his study. He plans his work. He keeps every book and paper in exact order and arrangement, so that what is needed may be found and used the moment it is needed.

So much for some personal excellences. But the man's chief charm comes in all his relations with others. And the basis of this lay in two simple things, that he understood men, and that he loved them. We often get these two things separately, but separately neither works perfection, and either alone sometimes works havoc. This man combined the two in a rare degree. He saw in others the good and evil that he found in himself and he cherished the good and forgave the evil.

That he abounded in mere external charity need hardly be said. In later life, at any rate, his means were plentiful and he gave of them freely. Many impositions were no doubt practiced upon him, but he had a clear eye as well as an open hand. 'Let me see your wound,' he said to an apparently crippled soldier. 'The sight might be disagreeable,' said the crippled soldier. 'I will try to bear it,' said the poet. 'If that is your spirit,' said the crippled soldier, 'I wish you a good morning.'

But Longfellow's charity went far deeper than

the open hand. He had the fullest appreciation of human weakness and an instinctive reluctance to expose or dwell upon or emphasize it. After a supper with many brilliant people, not probably censorious beyond the ordinary, he writes in his diary: 'General depreciatory tone about everything. I hate this.' Persons very generous with their money are often not generous with their time, and they sometimes embitter the gift by the manner of giving it. Owing to his great reputation, few men were more afflicted with bores than Longfellow. And he knew a bore when he saw one, scented the dry and soporific odor afar off. Of the terrible Count Gurowski he remarks, in his intimate record: 'We all feel as if a huge garden-roller had gone over us. He has a fifty-ogre power of devouring time.' Yet the counts and the other bores came again and sent their friends, so gentle and so ample was the poet's humanity.

It was not that he had not power of resistance or lacked a keen discrimination between good and bad, wise and foolish, profitable and frivolous. He can write, when occasion really calls for it, a harsh and biting judgment, like the following: '—— has published a poem (?) — most rabid trash, trash with a tin pail tied to its tail.' Yet his general tone toward the frailty and error of humanity is one of the largest comprehension and the most patient tolerance, and he rarely, if ever, violated the spirit of his own noble and beautiful counsel to a friend: 'Pray, don't let those unpleasant thoughts haunt and torment you. Dismiss them from your mind as disagreeable guests. Not the wrongs done to us harm us, only those we do to others.'

And if he had tenderness for even the bores and trouble-makers of the world, how much greater was his tenderness for those bound to him by ties of blood and ties of spiritual affinity! His love for the young wife he so early lost and for the other who shared his best years is shown by many an allusion in both prose and verse. We need not go far in his writing to discover his extreme sympathy with children and his delight in them. Occasional touches of petulant candor as to the drawbacks necessarily incident to work done at home only seem to emphasize the general attitude. Thus, he writes, with his charming, genial humor, 'Bought two velocipedes for the boys, who made a great noise with them in the morning, riding through the hall. Saturday is a bad day to buy playthings for children.' Which does not detract in the least from the grace and witchery of the following: 'My little girls are flitting about my study, as blithe as two birds. They are preparing to celebrate the birth-day of one of their dolls, and on the table I find this programme, in E.'s handwriting, which I purloin and send you, thinking it may amuse you. What a beautiful world this child's world is! So instinct with life, so illuminated with imagina-tion! I take infinite delight in seeing it go on around me.'

Longfellow's genius for friendship is almost

proverbial. Many of the noted men of his time —
Sumner, Felton, Lieber, Agassiz, Emerson, Lowell,
Norton, and many more not noted — loved him
and were beloved by him, with a sweet and peculiar
tenderness. I will not say that they all knew him
intimately, because it was not his nature to be
known intimately. But I do not think one of them
ever felt undue secretiveness on his part or anything but perfect openness and candor. It was
simply that he could not intrude his deepest feelings
even upon those who knew him best. And no appeal for sympathy, no demand upon his time for
interest, or attention, or advice, was ever met
with anything but the warmest and most entire
response. How the whole heart of friendship glows
in this vivid figure, conveying affection in a letter
to a friend: 'Did you ever, in a circus, see a man
leap through a paper balloon, tearing his way before
him, and falling into the arms of an associate? If
you have, then have you some image faint and
feeble of the manner in which my heart comes
tearing through this letter (as you break the seal)
to fall upon yours. Receive it gently, do not let it
fall to the ground.'

With his friends, as with humanity generally,
Longfellow was keen of vision. Their faults did not
escape his notice and in the privacy of his diary he
sometimes records them. 'Dined with ——. He
seems to me much my friend, and I like him — all
save his confounded positive way about everything.' Nothing can be more curious than his

frequent references to Sumner, whom he loved and who loved him. Longfellow evidently understands all his friend's numerous deficiencies, makes it plain that he does, but always with a touch so gentle that the deficiencies seem about to be turning into virtues. And against the criticism of others, even just, he has ready some defense of kindly sympathy or human comprehension.

To a being so affectionately constituted society was naturally attractive. He did not indeed seek large and promiscuous gatherings: 'I like intimate footings; I do not care for general society.' Nor did he shun long hours of solitude, either with Nature or with his own thoughts. But a company of two, or three, or a dozen, whom he knew and cherished, was delightful to him. He was not usually a great talker himself, being contented with an apt word in the right place. But he liked good wit, good wine, good fare, entered with the most delicate zest into the mellow atmosphere of such temperate conviviality as Milton commends to 'Lawrence, of virtuous father virtuous son.' How charming, from just this social point of view, is the comment of the restless Ruskin, 'Strange, that both you and Norton come as such *calm* influences to me and others.' How doubly charming this, when combined with the festive exhilaration of a picture painted by Lieber, in 1843: 'A delightful dinner at young Perkins's with Hillard, Longfellow, Sumner, Greene, etc. A right charming day — fine wine, fine moonshine, fine country-seat — and we actually put flowers in our hair.' 'Flowers in our hair,' especially in Sumner's, is irresistible!

II

As you read this account and many others similar, you are tempted to say, 'It is easy enough for anybody to be a saint, or something like one, when life is all roses and moonshine and tenderness and laughter.' Viewed in the broad aspect, Longfellow's life does seem to have been a peculiarly happy and fortunate one, one that offered little excuse for ill-nature or repining. He was born in a small New England city, and small New England cities are charming places, some of them. His family was sufficiently well-to-do to assure him leisure in pursuing the occupations he delighted in. He became a college professor at an age when most students now are beginning the drudgery of the doctorate with a professorship ten years away, and he relinquished teaching as soon as it became seriously irksome. He married once delightfully, and a second time even more delightfully, and had numerous children who gave him infinite content. He was able to follow the vocation that most attracted him and in that vocation he was successful from the very outset, without failure or difficulty, or hardly even struggle. He had a most attractive home, and could leave it substantially when the fancy seized him.

He had the finest possible taste for all the pleasures of life and had sufficient — not excessive —

liberty to indulge them. We have seen him in society. For art his appreciation was as delicate as it was varied. He was at home in all literature, could own rare books, and read them, and did. He loved the other arts, also, as a connoisseur, knew painting and sculpture and architecture and studied them all over Europe. Music meant more to him than to many literary men. And when the beauty of man's creation failed him, he could always turn to Nature and find ever new delight in the song of birds and the motion of clouds and stars.

The pleasure that came to him from his profession of literature was probably as great and as unalloyed as ever came to any man from such a source. He felt keenly, as every creator does, the enthusiasm, the rapturous exhilaration, of seeing desired beauty grow under his hands. Again and again he speaks of the delight of his work, the fascination of his subjects, the immense contentment of adding the perfecting touches which thrill dead substance into life. Things have gone a little wrong in the publication of *Hyperion*. 'No matter,' he says, 'I had the glorious satisfaction of writing it.'

And it was not often that anything went wrong about publication. For few authors, and especially few poets, have found their work so profitable from a material point of view. Editors courted him, publishers favored him. Even in the early days he could always get a few dollars for a few stanzas, though dollars were then scarce and stanzas common, as they have always been. Later, the few dollars became hundreds.

What is even dearer to poets than dollars, glory, was showered freely, and likewise from the very beginning. The fact is keenly and constantly noted, though without one trace of vanity or unseemly self-congratulation. 'The poem *Keramos* has gone to the Harpers, who will harp it in one hundred and fifty thousand households, or say half a million ears — if they will listen to such music as comes from a potter's wheel.' One thinks of the thousands of poets dead and gone whose verses were not harped in any households at all, and realizes that Longfellow's amiable disposition had much to favor it.

Also, besides these great sources of happiness, he had the fortunate temperament which makes pleasure out of little things, to others indifferent or even tedious. Life turned its sunny side to him, which, when all is said and done, is surely the greatest of felicities. 'Human life,' he says, 'is made up mostly of a series of little disappointments and little pleasures. The great wonder-flowers bloom but once in a lifetime; as marriage and death.' He might have added that there is an instinctive alchemy for turning common dust into little precious pleasures and that he himself was master of it. 'Another golden autumnal morning. Translated Anacreon's *Grasshopper* — an exquisite ode. A dream day.' Dream days, spun out of such fragile tissue as golden mornings and grasshoppers, are within the reach of all of us, might sweeten all our tempers, if we were alive to them.

This gentle, winning optimism of Longfellow is charmingly illustrated by a little comparison with Pepys, who was himself no pessimist and made dream occasions out of various pretty little odes of his own. Yet he goes to a wedding and his comment is: 'Strange, what delight we married people have to see these poor fools decoyed into our condition, every man and woman gazing and smiling at them.' Longfellow remarks, under similar circumstances: 'I like to go to weddings, and be married over again, as it were. It freshens our feelings.' Such is the difference in temperaments, which is more accountable than anything else for the happiness and the unhappiness of life.

It must not for one moment be supposed, however, that Longfellow was one of those fatuous optimists who shut their eyes to reality. Like the rest of us, he had his hours of complete dissatisfaction with the blessings that came to him. 'Worked, walked, and wished for many things,' is one of the brief and pregnant entries in his diary. He even expresses discontent with the rare good fortune of early success, which so many authors long for in vain. 'For my part, I have been meditating on the great importance it is to a literary man to remain unknown till he gets his work fairly done. It can hardly be overstated.'

Moreover, the poet had his positive trials and misfortunes, some of them, perhaps, not serious in themselves, yet such as have often served others as an excuse for ill-nature and complaint. To begin with, during a large part of his life he was a teacher, and teaching, however noble and satisfying in its aims, is wearing in its practice, especially to a nervous and sensitive temperament. He felt the drag of it, the tediousness of contracting your thoughts and adapting your ideas to those whose compass is narrow and their response limited: 'Perhaps the worst thing in a college life is this having your mind constantly a playmate for boys — constantly adapting itself to them, instead of stretching out and grappling with men's minds.' He felt the drag of set days and hours, the necessity of subordinating the wide sweep of his imagination to the systematic round of regular lessons and oft-repeated tasks. 'A delicious spring day! How I long to break from my moorings and be away! The weight and work of the college is crushing me. It is not the labor, but the being bound hand and foot, the going round and round in the treadmill that oppresses me. Air, air, more air! more freedom!'

So much for his necessary work of teaching. In his chosen work of literature, even he could not altogether escape the evils that beset everyone. 'A literary man leads an agreeable life only after he is dead,' said Voltaire. To make a man persist steadily in the pursuit of that most inconstant will o' the wisp, fame, through outward obstacles of indifference and rivalry, through inward obstacles of distraction and indolence, there must be the sting of the pestilent gadfly, ambition. I had almost said that that sting drives a man farther on his way than intellectual power or spiritual grace. Well, Longfellow, tranquil and balanced as he was by nature, felt the sting profoundly in his youth. 'The fact is, I most eagerly aspire after eminence in literature; my whole soul burns most ardently for it, and every earthly thought centres in it.' In later years he sometimes disclaims such ardor. Yet till extreme old age he labored on, toiling after a new and richer beauty, something that should more enrapture others and better satisfy himself. I believe that to the end the gadfly was still there, stinging, stinging.

Now, a life so stung is full and active, and with outward success it may be happy, but it has its great and serious drawbacks. There are moments of ecstasy, when limitless visions open before you, so rich and so abundant that words will not contain them, much less fingers write them down. There are dull and barren moments, when what you have achieved seems worthless and what you would achieve impossible. And Longfellow knew these swift, unhinging alternations, as others have known them.

There are external difficulties, also, all the more vexatious because of their pettiness. The whole world knows what a hell that stinging gadfly made Carlyle's life, because cocks crew, and organs played, and fools asked idle questions. Longfellow had no such morbid susceptibility. Yet even he was often driven to despair by the tormenting trifles that beset him. Bores haunted him daily, nightly. Good friends, even, had a habit of becoming bores when work was to be done. If he looked forward to a long morning of uninterrupted reflection and activity, there were swarms of letters knocking at his conscience when pressing intruders were not knocking at the door. 'All my hours and days go to perishable things. College takes half the time; and other people, with their interminable letters and poems and requests and demands, take the rest. I have hardly a moment to think of my own writings, and am cheated of some of life's fairest hours. This is the extreme of folly; and if I knew a man, far off in some foreign land, doing as I do here, I should say he was mad.'

Then there are the critics, a poisonous and inhuman generation, all the more annoying to popular authors whose works sell by thousands and are read by millions. It is just as easy to say that your work is worthless because you succeed as because you fail, and it hurts just as much. You may stop your ears and shut your eyes, avoid criticism altogether, as Longfellow professed to do, and make-believe that you have not a hostile reader in the world. But when Margaret Fuller derides you and Edgar Allan Poe accuses you of plagiarism, you know it and suffer from it, however you may forgive them with sunny and gentle charity.

Also, one critic cannot be shunned, or avoided, or silenced: yourself. There are times when he stands by you nobly and bids the world go hang. But just when you need his comfort most, he is apt to turn upon you, and say, as to Longfellow, of *Evangeline*, 'Alas, how difficult it is to produce anything really good! Now I see nothing but the defects of my work. I hope the critics will not find so many as I do.'

And the widest glory, when you have achieved it, million-mouthed glory, too often seems pale and empty and miserably inadequate to repay the effort and the suffering: 'Then we go to the museum. The play, wretched stuff. A young woman in yellow satin, representing the fashionable life of New York, holds a red-covered book, which she says is her "dear Henry W. Longfellow's poems"; and she asks her milliner which she prefers, Longfellow or Tennyson!'

Nor was Longfellow's apparently fortunate life free from the disasters which sooner or later make almost every human life a burden. Though he reached old age, and was exempt from serious maladies, he was constantly plagued by the ills that afflict sensitive temperaments and sedentary pursuits. He himself writes to Sumner, begging pardon for the insult — it certainly was one — that he does not see how any human being with a heart and a brain can ever be perfectly well. Keen and stinging neuralgias torment him for days and even months. Dyspepsia is a frequent guest, and, in his own opinion at any rate, makes him petulant and irritable.

HENRY WADSWORTH LONGFELLOW

Besides these comparatively minor evils, which, however, spoil more saints than the great sorrows of the world, Longfellow had to meet one of the sudden and terrible catastrophes that call for every ounce of manliness long training can store up. As the result of a trivial accident, his dearly loved wife was burned beyond recovery, under his very eyes, and even in his arms. Souls petted and cosseted by Fortune out of their native vigor are apt to fail in circumstances like these, to lose their energy of reaction, even if they do not settle into whining misery. Not so Longfellow. He rarely spoke of his grief, not to his nearest friends, not in the intimate pages of his diary. How deep and keen it was is shown by his quick reply to one who hoped he might be enabled to bear his cross: '*Bear* the cross, yes; but what if one is stretched upon it?' Yet the smooth stream of his life flowed on in its outward tranquillity. He did his work. He met men and women with the same gentle kindness he had always shown them.

For under the gentleness and tranquillity there was good measure of the rude strength that came from New England stock and Puritan habit. In face of a great moral ordeal, even of stern danger, who can doubt that the man would have been as firm and patient as a hero or a martyr? His nerves might have quivered and shuddered, but the something that is back of the nerves would have been absolutely unmoved. 'Yesterday I was at Mount Auburn and saw my own grave dug; that is, my tomb. I assure you, I looked quietly down into it, without one feeling of dread.' Minds of this temper may be caressed by Fortune, they cannot be spoiled by her.

The spiritual vigor was not wholly passive or attuned only to endurance. There was plenty of action in it, plenty of movement, plenty of endeavor. In extreme youth the poet practiced pugilism against a dummy of his own devising, much after the fashion of the excellent Oliver Proudfute in *The Fair Maid of Perth*. I am not aware that this led to any combative results in later years, but we see the same spirit, when he declares, 'activity — constant, ceaseless activity — that is what I need.' From the nature of his life the spiritual effort more often took the form of control, and it is evident that his outward serenity was in many cases the consequence of victory in a tempestuous inner struggle. Sometimes, however, as in his references to slavery and other moral wrongs, there is an outburst of violent indignation. And one entry in his diary is especially interesting as bearing traces of a spiritual conflict involving deep emotion and stern determination to accomplish a necessary result: 'This has been to me a day of indescribable mental suffering. I have given great pain to others; but I could not do otherwise and be true to myself. God grant it may be for the best.'

So, everywhere in diary and letters you catch glimpses, under the superficial serenity, of quick and petulant nerves that danced with joy or sorrow. You have to look carefully, for, as he himself says, 'with me all deep impressions are silent ones. I like to live on, and enjoy them, without telling those around me that I do enjoy them.' Yet the nerves gleam through. He holds a college examination and some dull face, an awkward gesture, or frivolous word annoys him: 'How sensitive I am to the appearance of my scholars!' He visits Niagara, and what to others is merely a curious spectacle fills him with strange uneasiness and almost suffering: 'Niagara is too much for me; my nerves shake like a bridge of wire; a vague sense of terror and unrest haunts me all the time. My head swims and reels with the ceaseless motion of the water.' Again, you think he is floating along easily on the current of his fortune, doing the same pleasant things today as yesterday, and entirely content to do them. And you come upon this outburst of gypsy waywardness, in the full spirit of old Fletcher's vagrant verses,

> Let rogues be staid that have no habitation.
> A gentleman may wander.

'I chanced to cast my eyes this morning upon a map of Italy, on which my old route was marked in red — the red vein of my young life-blood. Instantly I was mad for travel. It is spring, and the sun shines bright; and it seems a waste of life to stay here.' Such things make a Cambridge professor seem like a human being, do they not?

HENRY WADSWORTH LONGFELLOW

As Longfellow's tranquillity has misled some critics in regard to his capacity for emotion, so it has deceived others as to his depth of thought. Certainly he was not one to wear himself out by day and night in wrestling with difficult philosophical problems. But his intelligence was clear, accurate, and persistent. He was a close and careful scholar in his special fields of literature and language, and during his first trip abroad devoted himself with faithful study to acquiring the speech of the countries he visited. He was a very wide and discriminating, if not a very systematic, reader, and penetrated more deeply into the world's thinking than some who talk a great deal more about it. No man could have grappled so closely with Dante's *Paradiso* who had not an acute, as well as an energetic, intellect.

So with religion. This same, untroubled spirit kept in general a broad and hopeful outlook upon the spiritual struggles that went on around him. His optimism, as we have seen, was by no means of the blind or foolish variety, but it was solid and above all fruitful. That it was not always unshaken, however, is shown by his remark to a friend, who persisted in discussing

> Fixed fate, free will, foreknowledge absolute,
> And found no end, in wandering mazes lost.

'I told him that in general I was pretty quiet and calm in regard to these matters, and troubled only when at times a horrible doubt cut into the cool, still surface of my soul, as the heel of a skater cuts into smooth ice.'

Finally, in Longfellow's spiritual life, as in other phases of his character and career, I think we must note, perhaps rather vaguely, the perfecting touch of what I should call distinction, a delicate refinement which does not belong to all American authors, and which should be cherished in proportion to its rarity. This is the more valuable, because it implies not one atom of snobbishness or aristocratic exclusiveness. As I have already said, there never lived a man more thoroughly imbued with the essential principle of democracy — that is, the belief, the native, instinctive conviction, that the elements of resemblance in all human beings are far more important than the elements of difference. Yet with this fundamentally democratic sense Longfellow managed to combine the fineness of nature which is supposed to be a gift of aristocratic breeding. Just what I mean is admirably indicated in Howells's account of the poet's bearing on a social occasion. 'He did not talk much himself, and I recall nothing that he said. But he always spoke both wisely and simply, without the least touch of pose, and with no intention of effect, but with something that I must call quality, for want of a better word.' *Quality*, as here used, is perhaps indefinable. But every reader of Longfellow's life will realize what Howells means.

HENRY WADSWORTH LONGFELLOW

It is not my purpose, in these portraits of authors, to attempt literary criticism. At the same time, a man's character is intimately bound up with his work in life, and is often best illustrated by it. Thus, when writing of military figures, though admitting an incompetence for deciding technical questions, I found it necessary to refer to what great soldiers had done in their chosen career and to what in my judgment they had failed to do. A similar consideration of literary achievement, confined as far as possible to the psychographic standpoint, is quite essential.

I confess, then, that it puzzles me to find in Longfellow's character this marked element of distinction, or as Howells terms it, 'quality,' which seems to me to be conspicuously lacking in his poetry. It is true that all critics do not agree about this. Lowell, speaking in connection with the Westminster Abbey bust, affirmed that Longfellow's poetry had not only simplicity but distinction, and especially of recent years writers of high repute have reaffirmed Lowell's judgment, insisting upon the marked poetical merit of later work like the *Tales of a Wayside Inn* and many of the sonnets. Yet I cannot help thinking that these favorable estimates are affected partly by the poet's character and partly by a particular element of his work to be referred to shortly, and that most of those who read widely and critically will admit at once that the verse of Longfellow, with some excellent qualities, simplicity, sincerity, facility, freshness, grace, does lack just that element of distinction which is important to make poetry count from the literary point of view. In short, these readers, if they were pushed to it, would confess that they found the bulk of Longfellow's poetry rather commonplace; not common with any implication of vulgarity, or such positive defect — it is as far as possible removed from being that — simply commonplace, without peculiar quality to elevate it as literature above the average of intelligent writing; that is, without distinction.

I am not going to attempt to illustrate this. Most readers who habitually dwell with the great poets of the world can turn to almost any page of Longfellow and feel what I mean. Yet I will make one suggestion, which may help. In Stevenson's *Child's Garden of Verses* there are two slight, well-known lines, eminently marked with what I mean by distinction:

> This world is so full of a number of things,
> I'm sure we should all be as happy as kings.

If Longfellow had written those lines, I venture to assert that he would have used the word 'beautiful' instead of the words 'a number of.' The couplet would then be perfect Longfellow, and all distinction would have gone out of it.

Perhaps I should not have said that the lack of distinction in Longfellow's verse, when distinction was so notable an element in his character, puzzled me. We know, of course, that many persons of the finest artistic temperament could never do fine work. But then they do not try to do it. To have such a temperament, to have apparently the keenest sensitiveness to the distinction of others' work, and then to do work one's self of an entirely inferior order — this is what is puzzling — or would be if we did not see it happen in the history of art over and over again. And still I find it puzzling.

The most curious case in this regard, with Longfellow, is the translation of Dante. Of all the poets who have ever lived, Dante is the one who has the quality of distinction most. Longfellow knew this perfectly well, and spent years in endeavoring to transfer Dante's distinction into English, and failed utterly, and was not in the least aware of it. On the contrary, he triumphed in having conveyed, as he expressed it, 'the truth, the whole truth, and nothing but the truth,' whereas what he conveyed was the shell, the mere husk, dried apples, withered leaves; the same, yet the same with the informing life and spirit utterly vanished. Who that remembers the four lines which stand among the greatest tragic poetry of the world, can read Longfellow's rendering of them without a shudder?

> Whenas we read of the much-longed-for smile
> Being by such a noble lover kissed,
> This one, who ne'er from me shall be divided,
> Kissed me upon the mouth all palpitating.

And so I have heard some persons say, after a prolonged dose of Longfellow's poetry, 'Really, anybody could have written it.' Which sets one reflecting, because if anybody could have written it, anybody would, and the world would be flooded with *Evangelines* and *Hiawathas*.

There are, I think, two elements that account chiefly for Longfellow's immense literary success. One is technical. It is simply that he had the power of telling a story in verse. This was the strong point of the much-despised Victorians, and, after unduly contemning it for a generation, the world shows signs of returning to it. It is something the great poets often lack and writers of a very inferior order abound in. Lope de Vega had it far more than Shakespeare. Dumas had a similar gift in prose far more than Balzac or Flaubert. The great Georgian poets, Coleridge, Shelley, Keats, were utterly unable to tell a simple story effectively. Longfellow, on the other hand, understood how to hold his reader from beginning to end. He is often called diffuse, though he himself hated diffuseness and what he termed 'watered poetry.' From this point of view of narrative interest, he is not diffuse. Every detail helps to fix and hold and carry forward the reader's attention.

This is just as true of the shorter poems and ballads as of the longer narratives. The briefest lyric seizes some simple, genuine phase of human feeling and presents it in a dramatic fashion which is certain to touch the heart. That Longfellow knew perfectly well what he was aiming at and exactly how to achieve it is shown most curiously by a passage in one of his earlier letters, referring to the *Wreck of the Hesperus*: 'I think I shall write more. The *national ballad* is a virgin soil here in New England; and there are great materials. Besides, I have a great notion of working upon the *people's* feelings.'

The other justification for Longfellow's glory is far more important than any mere secret of dramatic technique. It is simply that his poetry reflects many of the rare and beautiful qualities we have discovered in the study of his character. The distinction may be absent, but the sweetness, the gentleness, the noble effort, the devoted self-sacrifice, the broad and tolerant optimism, the lofty hope — all these are manifested in his verses, all these, to a greater or less extent, must pass into the hearts of his readers. And when you consider what and how many those readers are, you will wonder whether any poet in the world before ever had such a glorious opportunity. Certainly not Homer or Dante, and hardly even Shakespeare, speaks to men as Longfellow speaks. His verses are on millions of tongues at an age when the tongue and the ear are in their closest contact with the heart. And who shall say that any of those great poets is on the whole more fitted to be master of such a mighty and pervading influence?

It is a great thing to have a beautiful soul. It is a far, far greater thing to leave that soul as an eternal possession and example and inspiration to millions of one's fellow-men.

III
WALT WHITMAN

CHRONOLOGY

WALT (WALTER) WHITMAN
  Born, Huntington, Long Island, May 31, 1819.
  Varied life, largely journalistic, Long Island, and New
    York till 1848.
  Editor *Brooklyn Eagle*, 1846–1848.
  In New Orleans, 1848.
  Leaves of Grass published, 1855.
  Varied work and existence till 1873.
  In Camden, 1873–1892.
  Died, Camden, March 20, 1892.

WALT WHITMAN

III

WALT WHITMAN *

I

HE WAS a man of the plain people, if anybody knows what that means. At any rate, he liked to boast of it. He had the education of circumstances, the training of broad human contact, the discipline of hard facts. In his boyhood he wandered over the pastures and beaches of Long Island. Later, he wandered more widely, physically and mentally, looking into manifold eyes, touching manifold hands, kissing manifold lips, forgetting more faces than many of us ever see. 'I envy you your capacity for being at home with anybody in any crowd,' said the home-keeping Emerson. He liked the solitude of vast throngs as much as he liked the solitude of starry nights. He liked the bustle, the restless, creative activity, the hurried speech, the whirr, of busy modern America. 'I see how lucky

* The worship of Whitman is so zealous that Whitman material accumulates with astonishing rapidity, and a considerable amount has appeared since this portrait was written. Perhaps the most notable volumes are *The Uncollected Prose and Poetry of Walt Whitman*, collected and edited by Emory Holloway, and *The Gathering of the Forces*, a reprint of Whitman's early writing in the *Brooklyn Eagle*, edited by Messrs. Rodgers and Black. Both these collections develop and emphasize interesting aspects of Whitman's earlier career and production. Nevertheless, I do not think anything has appeared or will appear to alter seriously the fundamental elements of his character as I have attempted to delineate them.

I was that I was myself thrown out early upon the average earth — to wrestle for myself — among the masses of people — never living in coteries; that I have lived cheek by jowl with common people.'

He was literary by nature; that is, he had from youth the double instinct of feeling and expressing, which comes from Heaven knows where, and the instinct of expressing was fostered by early and abundant journalistic practice. In his youthful days the literary tendency showed itself in more or less conventional verses and in a considerable amount of not especially distinguished prose. Later, it occurred to him that, as he was a man of the people, why should he not be the poet of the people? He was a democrat, he was an American. Democracy and America had secrets that had never been uttered, great truths as yet unknown, vast possibilities, vast hopes, vast treasures of physical and spiritual delight. Someone must give these things adequate expression. Why not he? Literature had existed hitherto for literary classes, had represented a narrow culture, a limited experience, a selfish hope. Now it should take in the whole world. He had known and loved the common toilers and sufferers. Out of his knowledge and sympathy he would speak for them: 'I have made my poetry out of actual, practical life,' he said, 'such as is common to every man and woman, so that all have an equal share in it.' And again, 'I am willing to think I represent vast averages and the

generic American masses — that I am their voice.'
He aimed to write a 'Poem of the People — representing the people, so copious, so simple, so fierce.'
His admirers called *Leaves of Grass* 'the Bible of
Democracy,' and he never showed any disposition
to contradict them — quite the opposite.

He wanted to break entirely with older forms of
literature, to eschew them, to forget them, wanted
to drop traditions, conventions, and establish a
technique as novel as he thought his matter was.
He worked hard for years, he says, to eliminate
set phrases, those stereotyped poetical figures which
lost their sparkle and freshness a thousand years
ago. Literature? What is it? He neither knows nor
cares. Life is good enough for him. 'The more the
literary guild discuss me, the more I seem outside
the particular interest they chew upon with such
relish.' 'I hate literature... I do not love a literary
man as a literary man.'

But all this is as old as literature itself. Strong,
rising authors are apt to declare that they have
done with literature. The preoccupation of novelty,
of doing something altogether different, is one of the
surest marks of the literary instinct, and the
classics represent the revolts that have survived
amid the million wrecks of revolts that have been
neither literature nor anything else . There is even
about Whitman the peculiar literary consciousness,
the uneasy sense of the judgment and criticism of
literary men that comes from being half-educated
or self-educated. He is not one, like Villon, who has

passed light-heartedly from learning to vagabond-age, but one who has toiled upward from vagabond-age to learning or literature, and never feels quite secure of his position. We see in Shakespeare just the same result of a book education that has been imperfect and incomplete. This it is that accounts for Shakespeare's stupefaction before the hidden possibilities of words, his curious jugglings with them, his naïve admiration of his own verbal pyrotechnics. To Whitman, also, words, which ring so hollow to the trained man of letters, were delightful mystical entities, dainty playthings to forget life with, bubbles to toss in the air and to watch delightedly as they sparkled in the summer sunshine. Only so can we explain his fearful deal-ings in such polyglot monstrosities as *Americanos, camerados, Santa Spirita*, his *résumés, eidolons, libertads*, etc. These things do not constitute a style, but a lingo.

Thus, Whitman's literary attitude had too much theory behind it to be really popular, really repre-sentative of democracy. It was not spontaneous enough. Lanier's harsh criticism, that all the elaborate rough garb and slovenly carriage were merely inverted dandyism, and that Whitman's poetry was everywhere 'posing to see if it cannot assume a naïve and striking attitude,' is much exag-gerated, but has a basis of truth. Just as Zola used the brute vice of democracy to make a literary reputation, so, in much the same spirit, Whitman used its brute virtue.

WALT WHITMAN

The real literature of the people, as we find it in the old ballads, for instance, sung right out of the heart of the people, is altogether different. It uses literary machinery and conventional forms quite unconsciously and just because they are conventional — and therefore natural. Above all, it presents the spirit of the people in a fashion totally different from Whitman's. It insists, not upon what the common people are, but upon what they are not — but would like to be. Here is the fundamental error of Whitman's attempt to be the poet of democracy. He endeavors to represent men's common life, glorified, indeed, transfigured, but glorified in overalls and transfigured through sweat, mud, grime, and weariness. Now of all human societies democracy has least desire to see itself as it is. An aristocratic, worldly class is not unwilling to behold even its vices travestied, takes a cynical pleasure in the process, saying, 'See here, such I am, but after all I am the fine flower of culture and I would not be otherwise.' But a democracy, especially the American democracy, maintains a veritable conspiracy, in the press, in the pulpit, on the stage, for getting itself presented quite other than it is, for keeping all sorts of brutal facts rigidly and severely in the background. We want our stories, we want our plays, full of heroism, full of melodrama, full of the splendid things we always expect the other fellow to be doing. The plumber, the brakeman, does not want a poem describing the glory of a wiped joint, or a coupled freight-car, does not have his picture taken with a gasoline torch or a red lantern. He always sees himself in his best, ready-made Sunday suit, walking with his young woman in a bargain frock from a department store. But in Whitman's poems he is a plumber or a brakeman only. And the democratic instinct is herein entirely right, even according to Whitman himself. For the essence of democracy and all that can justify it is aspiration, and why aspire when we are patted on the back and told that we are perfect just as we are?

Further, democracy, our democracy, means women. Our primary education is controlled by women, our social life exists for women, our literature is adapted to women, our manners are dictated by women, our earnings are spent by women. Now Whitman's poems, whatever their excellences, are not women's poems. It is really pathetic to see his longing for recognition by the reading sex. Some women, some noble and beautiful women, like Mrs. Gilchrist, accept him fully. How pleased he is! 'I always say that it is significant when a woman accepts me.' Again, '*Leaves of Grass* is essentially a woman's book: the women do not know it, but every now and then a woman shows that she knows it.' Very few of them, and it will never be different. What women detest in Whitman is, not that he makes sex too prominent, but that he does not make it prominent enough. The modern woman, like the woman of all ages, knows perfectly well that sex is her supreme instrument of domination and she instinctively obtrudes it in social life in every possible way by the subtle suggestion which is far more effective than nudity. Whitman shows the bare fact of sex, in its cruel insignificance, and then tosses it into a corner. This is to rob woman of all her privileges, and she will not forgive it. Sex in literature, to woman, is sentiment, something forever tantalizing and never satisfying, a halo of the impossible about a nucleus of the prohibited. What democracy — that is, woman — demands in literature is what she delightfully calls 'a heart interest.' There is no heart interest in Whitman.

The true, the satisfying poet of democracy, as democracy is and will be, for many years to come, is Longfellow. Longfellow fixes our attenton not on what we are, but on what we might be. Longfellow makes gentle music of all those creditable emotions with which we like to believe this country is sprinkled, like a meadow with blossoms in May. Above all, Longfellow gives woman that exalted importance which is no doubt her due and which she now likes to have assigned her, not as a courtesy, but as an inalienable right.

Thus, the great poem of the people, the Bible of democracy, is not read by the people and will never be popular. It may be literature of the people and by the people. Literature for the people it is not. The plumber — that is, the plumber's young woman — will never read it, though she devours *Evangeline.* Earnest educators will never edit it in neat paper issues for the devout perusal of grammar scholars. *Children of Adam* will never be droned from graduation platforms on hot June nights, nor *Passage to India* ever be chosen to exhibit the peculiar oratorical gift which is to float James into the hospitable precincts of the Hall of Fame. Only, by that curious infelicity which picks a man's least characteristic work to typify him — *English Traits* for Emerson and *The Skylark* for Shelley — *My Captain* has continued to get a certain hold on the imagination of many who know nothing of its author. 'Damn *My Captain*!' said Whitman.

It is extremely curious to observe the poet's own attitude about this matter of his popularity. He has admirers in England, enthusiastic admirers, and some at home. Oh, yes, that is well. Their incense is thoroughly acceptable. And of course one does not want to be admired by the herd. 'Longfellow was the expresser of the common themes — of the little songs of the masses — perhaps will always have some vogue among average readers of English.' Certainly one would not wish to be anything like that. Yet when one writes for the herd —! And it is strange that the average reader does not understand. Our own mother and best lover does not understand — simply gives it up. Our dear friend, the honest, true-hearted brakeman, Peter Doyle, full of common sense and shrewd insight, loves us, but he cannot read our books. The devoted nurse of our old age tries hard to admire, reads a page or two, then takes a rest, and reads another. Well, it must be admitted, we 'are not

popular and never will be,' but we have written
Leaves of Grass, and *Leaves of Grass* is the Bible of
Democracy, just the same — for everybody but
democrats.

II

The above analysis of Whitman's relation to his
own work is an indispensable prelude to the discussion of the man, because the two are so constantly and inseparably intertwined with each
other. If, however, I have given the impression
that a certain artificiality and literary consciousness in the work extended altogether to the author,
I must hasten to dispel it. 'The great poets are to
be known by the absence in them of tricks and by
the justification of perfect personal candor,' wrote
Whitman himself, nobly. There may have been
tricks in his verse. There was perfect candor in his
heart. 'If I talk wrong, then I talk wrong — but
I talk honest, or always mean to: maybe that is the
chief thing, to talk honest.' It is, at any rate, a very
great thing.

By the industry and devotion of Whitman's
earnest admirers, we have material for the intimate
study of his life during a large portion of his career.
Let us take him in age first, for here we have one of
the most faithful and exhaustive records ever
preserved of the life of any man. Horace Traubel
far out-Boswelled Boswell in the patience and the
minuteness with which he chronicled his hero's
lightest words and vaguest gestures. I do not know

that he has quite equaled the excellent Bishop of Bellay, Camus, who, to make double assurance of veracity in writing the life of Saint Francis of Sales, bored a hole into the saint's room that he might be observed when he thought himself entirely alone. Perhaps this is going too far. At any rate, Traubel went far enough.

Really no human being before was ever so microscopically noted, so completely stripped of the decent garniture of privacy. And few would come out of the ordeal so well as Whitman. We see a serene, lovable old man looking back on his own great achievement, commenting leisurely on his failures and successes and on his vast and varied contact with human life. Intellectually these comments are marked by a never-failing curiosity and an immense desire to get at the truth of things. There is a hatred of partisanship, of narrow prejudice, of the greed of spiritual triumph, no matter how good or bad the cause may be. All Whitman's sympathies are with what are called radical and progressive ideas. Yet against any bitterness of advocacy, even for these things, he protests in a moment. He 'dissents from partisanship, whatever its name or form, for after the best the partisan will say, something better will be said by the man.'

A systematic and consistent thinker he was not. He had neither the training nor the intellectual intensity. But he occasionally struck out a casual reflection of wide significance, as in his doubt 'whether the Reformation of Luther was of such value to the world as most Protestants think.' And his critical remarks and brief characterizations have often an extraordinary shrewdness and felicity, as the summary of Swinburne, quoted by Professor Bliss Perry, 'Ain't he the damnedest simulacrum?' or the inimitable touching-off of Henry James, 'James is only feathers to me'; or the more serious portrayal of Sherman, 'Seamy, sinewy, in style — a bit of stern open air made up in the image of a man.'

But the mere intellectual attraction of this elaborately sketched figure would not carry us far. It is the love in it that counts, the genuine tenderness, unshaken by age, unsoured by fatigue and pain. Who has surpassed the beautiful humility of the confession, 'I no doubt deserved my enemies, but I don't believe I deserved my friends'? If long love deserves friends and forgiving charity and affection that caresses like sunlight, this man certainly deserved them. The undermining strain of tedious illness could not make him inconsiderate or forgetful. To the end he thought of those he loved more than of himself. And what sweet, simple, noble words he has which clearly come straight from the heart. 'It seems to be the notion of some people I should "select" my friends — accept and reject and so forth. Love, affection, never selects — just loves, is just affectionate.' Again 'W. kisses me good night. He said, "We are growing near together. That's all there is in life for people — just to grow near together."'

Also, this deep, unlimited tenderness was not confined to a narrow circle or to a few choice, sympathetic spirits. Not many men have responded so quickly and vividly to the mere human contact, have felt the voice and sight of man and woman as such so constantly delightful. Nothing brings him hope and happiness more completely than the presence of a joyous spirit. A radical boy orator, full of western hope, drifts into his room and drifts out again. 'Oh, he was a beautiful boy — a wonderful daybeam. I shall probably never see his face again — yet he left something here with me that I can never quite lose.' And such broad human affection was based on sympathy, on the ever-present sense that others felt what he felt and enjoyed what he enjoyed. It was thus that when he was tormented by restless, sleepless illness, and the Fourth of July racket began under his window, he checked every effort to interfere with it: 'Don't send them away, Mary: the boys don't like to be disturbed either. Besides, who knows but there may be a sicker man round the corner?'

There is no surer foundation for democracy than human tenderness like this, and because Whitman's democracy was built on such tenderness, it was broad and unfailing and indestructible. He occasionally notes faults and weaknesses in this great triumphant America of ours, notes them with a shrewdness which shows that he was by no means blind. But his general tone is one of enthusiastic confidence. These States hold the key to the future.

WALT WHITMAN

These States are the country of hope, the abiding-place of love, the breeding-ground of strong, fruitful virtues, which shall make the world over. The men and women of these States are the children of liberty, the nourishers of justice, the begetters of joy. It is not certain that democracy greatly needs to be told its excellences. If it does, Whitman should be the man for democracy.

And as this kindly, tranquil spirit looked out with confidence, from the bare refuge of his shrunken age, upon the seething conflict of the political world about him, so his vision of the moral and spiritual world was equally joyous and serene. They asked him if anything had ever shaken his faith in humanity. 'Never! Never! I trust humanity. Its instincts are in the main right.' And again, 'I never have any doubts of the future when I look at the common man.' So heroic was his trust, so indomitable his optimism, that he is said to have complained, 'Emerson's deficiency is that he doubts everything.' What must have been the robustness of that faith to which Emerson appeared a skeptic!

It is true that, as with all ardent optimists and pessimists alike, you sometimes get an impression of effort, of willful eye-shutting. In one unguarded moment Whitman admits, 'I have seen in the later years of my life exemplifications of devilishness, venom, in the human critter, which I could not have believed possible in my more exuberant years.' And elsewhere he recognizes, still more unguardedly, the slight touch of strain I have sug-

77

gested: 'Life is not so bright that anybody should wanton with it — should keep its shadows too much to the front.' But in the main, his spiritual contentment is unlimited. He overrides the little ills of life, sees through them, sees beyond them, helps others to see beyond them. He drowns pettiness, meanness, decay, even disgust, which sometimes will peer out from dark corners, in a great security of joy. Dogmatic religion he has no need of, never apparently felt or realized those torments which it fosters and appeases. 'I never, never was troubled to know whether I would be saved or lost: what was that to me?' But in the firm, calm, supporting assurance of the peace of God few men of our day have surpassed him: 'I claim everything for religion; after the claims of my religion are satisfied, nothing is left for anything else.'

It is sometimes asserted that Whitman lacked that very indefinable something called humor. If this means that he took himself and his work rather too seriously, it is just. If it means that he was not generally ready with witty, pungent speech, it is also just, though less so. What, for instance, could be better than his retort, when asked if he read Blaine's speeches, 'No, indeed — I've got too much respect for the clock.' But if humor is based in the cheerful, receptive, kindly attitude toward life which I have indicated, then Whitman had certainly his share of it. How admirably gentle in its raillery is the description of the Duyckink brothers: 'I met those brothers: they were both "gentlemenly men" — and by the way, I don't know any description that it would have pleased them better to hear — both very clerical-looking — thin — wanting in body: men of truly proper style, God help 'em!' How pleasant in its mirthful twinkle the tribute to the sacred calendar: 'I believe in saints, if they're far enough off.'

Will it be denied that Shakespeare's humor is so delightful because it is all sunshine? Well, Whitman was a sun-lover, also, liked long, naked drenchings of sunlight in green solitudes. He wanted all about him to be sunny, made it so. He said, 'Some people are so much sunlight to the square inch.' He was, and he loved those who were. He said of himself, 'I stand for the sunny point of view — stand for the joyful conclusions.' And of his book he used this phrase, which surely would not discredit the loveliest poem in the world, 'My book is written in the sun and with a gay heart.' What better motto could be inscribed on *Twelfth Night* or *As You Like It?*

Such is this gracious and alluring figure of an old man, which might do honor to the richest canvas of Rembrandt. If we must put some shadows in it, they are not deep ones. From the usual weaknesses of prolonged invalidism and incipient senility he seems exceptionally free. If he is at times garrulous, we must remember that no man's garrulity was ever before recorded so without pity. The absence of fretfulness, petulance, is really remarkable. The rare outbursts of indignation that occur are justified by the circumstances. He endured tedious intrusion and irrelevant questioning with a saintlike meekness, and it was only when he was bored past the patience of man that he burst out with what a friend so vividly described as his ' magnificent No!'

The charge of a rather flamboyant and offensive egotism is less easily disposed of. If you know Whitman, know his naïveté, his gentleness, his honesty, you do not mind the egotism. Besides, when a man so greatly and genuinely admires all the other works of God, why should he not bestow a little admiration on himself? At the same time, it must be admitted that the attitude evokes in most of us a kindly smile, in some a cumulative irritation. This he cannot understand. 'I talked of myself as I would of you; blamed and praised just the same; looked at myself just as if I was somebody else; I am not ashamed of it; I have never praised myself where I would not have praised somebody else.' There are spiritual complexities in this utterance which I need not analyze, but which no one can fail to enjoy. To be sure, he occasionally doubts himself — as a moral exercise: 'It takes a good deal of resolution to do it; yet it should be done — no one is safe until he can give himself such a drubbing: until he can shock himself out of his complacency.' But I question whether that robust complacency could have been shaken by any shock less than the electric chair. Even as regards his person, the twinkling complacency is not wholly absent. He offers one of his portraits to a lady in Washington. 'She said she'd rather have a picture that had more love in it. It's a little rough and tumble, possibly, but it's not a face I could hate. Could you? Honest Injun, Horace, could you hate it?' But as to his book — it is old, it is new, it is elemental, it is universal, it includes everything and everybody, it is outside all the classifications of the critics, has a place of its own, a mighty place. It will be read, it must be read, the heart of man needs it because it contains all the heart of man. And the assertion, made by so many poets, that he did not write it, but a higher power working through him, goes but little way to dim the self-satisfaction of authorship. Perfect appreciation and admiration of such a masterpiece naturally become the touchstone of mortality, and hence this man, whose love and sympathy were so broad, so catholic, at times appears exclusive in a way strangely inconsistent with his real democracy. There is too much about *us, our crowd.* Men seem sometimes to be divided into the damned and the elect on the mere basis of acceptance of the Whitman gospel.

For all these things there was, of course, much excuse in the atmosphere in which Whitman passed his later years. He was not widely praised, but he was immensely praised, and by those whose praise should exalt any man. To be applauded by minds so diverse as Emerson and Symonds, Dowden and Thoreau, to be idolized by men like O'Connor and women like Mrs. Gilchrist, was surely enough to turn the steadiest head. On the whole, I think we may affirm that Whitman kept his balance very sanely.

III

But the picture of the man in old age, freely and completely as it is developed in Horace Traubel's volumes, would be indeed inadequate. We must get what glimpses we can of him farther back, when the torch was full ablaze, when *Leaves of Grass* was inchoate, in the bud, slowly maturing through the fat richness of a vast, observant, many-sided experience of life. The lights that come to us are not so many as we could wish, but they are sometimes vividly, overwhelmingly definite.

There is the same egotism always, perhaps even more bristling and protuberant. If others will not praise my poems, I will praise them, vigorously — and anonymously. There is a certain lack of delicacy, an entire lack, Professor Perry calls it, as in the quite unscrupulous use of Emerson's private letter for advertising purposes.

There is a waywardness, a moodiness of temperament, inborn, and further fostered by vagrant habits of life and thought. 'Back of all else in me is feeling — emotional substance.' This shows rarely in violent temper, as in the thrashing of the sexton who forcibly removed the poet's hat, worn in thoughtless reminiscence of Quaker customs. It shows more often, modified, but not neutralized, by Dutch solidity and leisureliness, in a spirit of contradiction or of obstinate persistence. 'My dear mother used to say to me: "Walt — does thee not sometimes — just sometimes, Walt — look for differences where there are none?" Dear mother!' The persistence was now bound up with high things, now with less high. Sometimes it is an idol which 'seized upon me, made me its servant, slave; induced me to set aside other ambitions; a trail of glory in the heavens, which I followed, followed, with a full heart.' Sometimes it is a whim or slighter fancy, grasped and clung to with the same tenacity. 'When once I am convinced, I never let go.' And as there were moods of violence, so there were moods of quiet: 'I had, I may say, an unusual capacity for standing still, rooted on a spot, at a rest, for a long spell, to ruminate, hours in and out sometimes.'

But back of all these moods and anchoring them securely to reality, we must see, not the shattered physique of Traubel's volumes, but the splendid, vigorous, abundant, healthy temperament, so rare in poets and in literary men generally, the temperament that did not shrink from crowds or noises, or coarse odors, or harsh speech, that reveled instinctively in the surging pressure of city streets as in the driven solitude of wild sea beaches, that was at home everywhere, at peace everywhere, everywhere alike throbbing with the buoyant, joyous, intense vividness of simple life.

No one can understand Whitman who does not base such understanding on a sense of this perfect bodily health, this normal, sound adjustment of muscles, nerves, and organs, which remained entirely unbroken till after the shattering strain and exhaustion of his war endeavor. Everywhere in the reminiscences of his early days you catch the ring, the exultant ecstasy of abounding physical vigor, the eager response of eye and limb to any demand the heart can make on them. What a rhythm of gorgeous living throbs in this brief note, warm from actual experience! 'A solitary and pleasant sundown hour at the pond, exercising arms, chest, my whole body, by a tough oak sapling thick as my wrist, twelve feet high — pulling and pushing, inspiring the good air. After I wrestle with the tree awhile, I can feel the young sap and virtue welling up out of the ground and tingling through me from top to toe, like health's wine.'

And as the body was sound and healthy, so it was comely to look upon, which does not mar the joy of living in the least. Stalwart, well-proportioned, rubicund, with a clear, bright eye, and a noble bearing, the man, from youth to age, had a presence that attracted all beholders. You can see in the numerous photographs what the charm was, though I confess that in every one of them there is something about the eyes I cannot wholly like, something of the waywardness, pushed almost to insolence, perhaps accentuated by the rough and careless garb. Those who write from actual personal contact seem to register a magnetism greater than can be suggested by the photographs

WALT WHITMAN

'His presence exerted a peculiar fascination almost intoxicating,' writes one especially ardent admirer. And Lincoln, not an admirer, and not intoxicated, said of him passing in the street, as Napoleon said of Goethe, 'Well, *he* looks like a *man*.' There was mental sanity, also, that round, balanced, joyous courage and hope which are better served by a healthy body, though they do not always go with it. Just hear this simple note from a pleasant day's journey: 'On the Mary Powell, enjoyed everything beyond precedent.' He always did. He takes a quiet walk in the country. 'And there were the detours, too, wanderings off into the country out of the beaten paths; I remember one place in Maryland in particular to which we would go. How splendid above all was the moon — the full moon, the half moon; and then the wonder, the delight of the silences.' It is the ecstasy of a man who has no worn, dead nerve tissue to cloud the ample working of his spirit. Whitman himself lucidly defines the glory of such a state of exaltation. 'A man realizes the venerable myth — he is a god walking the earth, he sees new eligibilities, powers and beauties everywhere; he himself has a new eyesight and hearing. The play of the body in motion takes a previously unknown grace. Merely *to move* is then a happiness, a pleasure — to breathe, to see, is also.'

Out of this superabundance of health and physical vigor there no doubt came, in Whitman's early life, a freedom of living not wholly consonant with conventional standards of morals. A country which is perfectly contented that a man should have had a number of wives and no children, but shrieks when he has a number of children and no wife, will never accept nor condone the poet's unauthorized, though perhaps after all somewhat mythical, progeny. Yet such progeny is quite compatible with a much more normal sexual habit than obtains in many marriages. It may at least be asserted that Whitman was not fundamentally corrupt, or dissipated in any proper sense of the term, and the plain statement of Mrs. Stafford, with whom he boarded and who knew him, if anyone did, may set him squarely on his feet for any normal man — or woman: 'He is a good man; I think he is the best man I ever knew.'

This warmth of blood, this depth and energy and tenderness of affection, appear most charmingly in all the relations of life as well as in the sexual. 'What is humanity,' he says, 'in its faith, love, heroism, even morals, but *emotion?*' And more personally, 'How many's the time I've just lived for days and days practically on my affections alone!' Nowhere do we get a more delightful, winning idea of the man than in the series of letters written to his mother from Washington during the war, simple letters, almost illiterate in their naïve tenderness, full of thoughtful care and filial yearning and that patient interest in the details of a loved one's life which cannot be feigned and cannot be mistaken.

WALT WHITMAN

Also, there is the beautiful list of Whitman's male friendships, not indeed quite so lengthy as his enthusiastic talk of comradeship would lead us to believe, because many who loved him felt that they could not quite touch, could not quite understand. But the simplest souls came nearest to him. How charming is the attachment shown in his letters to the honest railroad man, Peter Doyle, who could not do much with *Leaves of Grass*, but had the deepest regard and admiration for its author! The demonstrative tenderness that accompanied these simple friendships of Whitman, the caressing and kissing and embracing, is unusual and noticeable and affords an ample field for analysts of Freudian propensities. To me it is interestingly compared with similar manifestations by one of the purest and noblest figures in American history, General Joseph E. Johnston, who was also accustomed to meet and part from his friends — for instance, General Lee — with such demonstrations as are exchanged between a lover and his beloved.

Nor was this depth of affection all subjective, all, so to speak, selfish. On the contrary, it welled out in thoughtfulness, kindness, sacrifice for others. The noblest, the most fruitful experience of Whitman's life, as he himself admitted, was his work in the Washington hospitals during the war. Living in the city at that time, he gradually became interested, without any official status, in the wounded soldiers, devoted long, long hours to them, watched with them, soothed them, comforted them, took the bulk of his small earnings to buy dainties for them, which he himself distributed with words more helpful than the dainties. No bitterer, more horrible record of wounds and death and the agony of war has ever been penned than Whitman's account of these hospital experiences. Sensitive as he was, susceptible as he was, he shrank from no shock or disgust of disease or operation, holding many a hand at the hour of death, though, as he says, he often trembled and fainted afterward at what he had heard and seen.

And what made his comfort and attendance so beautiful and so satisfying was that it was not a mere matter of duty, or charity, or even pity, but was warmed by the glow of real human, personal love. The sick and dying looked for him, longed for him, as for no one else. 'Come again, Walt!' they cried; 'Oh, Walt, be sure to come again!' Why they felt so is easily seen when we read only one of the many letters in which Whitman expresses his affection. 'Sometimes, after an interval, the thought of one I much love comes upon me strong and full all of a sudden — and now as I sit here by a big open window, this beautiful afternoon, everything quiet and sunny — I have been and am now, thinking so of you, dear young man, and of your love, or more rightly speaking, our love for each other — so curious, so sweet, I say so *religious* — we met there in the Hospital — how little we have been together — seems to me we ought to be some together every day of our lives — I don't care about talking or amusement, but just to be together, and work together, or go off in the open air together.' This is the tone that goes to men's hearts, whether in hospitals or prisons or palaces, or heaven or hell.

IV

But thus far we have been dealing with a prosaic Whitman, a prose Whitman, at any rate. We must not forget that we are studying, not only a man, but a great poet, one of the great poets of the world, who put original, and perhaps even novel thoughts into an original and novel form. What an advantage they have, these poets, over the common herd of us. All the aspirations, all the hopes, all the ideals, which we can only mutter or murmur, with strangled inarticulateness, they can sing right out with unimagined glory. Nay, even those dull strains which in us seem earthly and to be hidden, they can transfigure and illumine, making all things mortal splendid just because they are mortal and yours and mine as well as theirs. Thus *Leaves of Grass*, with all its various folds and gleaming tissues, is a colossal autobiography, not of the poet only, but of you and me and every man. Its egotism, often loud and brazen, is egotism for all of us.

What am I after all but a child, pleas'd with the sound of my
    own name? repeating it over and over,
I stand apart to hear — it never tires me.
To you your name also;
Did you think there was nothing but two or three pronuncia-
    tions in the sound of your name?

WALT WHITMAN

Its lofty, challenging self-assurance is the self-assurance of the mighty seers, striking the taproot of their hearts deep, deep down into the greater heart of man.

> I am that I am, and they that level
> At my abuses reckon up their own,

says Shakespeare; and Petrarch,

> Intenda mi chi puo, ch'i'm' intend io.

And Whitman,

> Leave my works,
> And go lull yourself with what you can understand, and with piano-tunes,
> For I lull nobody, and you will never understand me.

How the bodily health and vigor leap out in singing verses, with their exuberant felicity!

> And who has been happiest? I think it is I — I think no one was ever happier than I.

> And henceforth I will go celebrate anything I see, or am,
> And sing and laugh and deny nothing

Also, the red thread of sensibility, of emotion, of affection and tenderness, gleams and glistens through the whole fabric, sometimes subtly evading, sometimes triumphant and irresistible.

> O what is it in me that makes me tremble so at voices?
> Surely whatever speaks to me in the right voice, him or her I shall surely follow,
> As the wave follows the moon, silently, with fluid steps everywhere around the globe.

Who has ever put more sympathy into one line than throbs in the following, of the poet?

He is no arguer, he is judgment (Nature accepts him absolutely),
He judges not as the judge judges but as the sun falling round
  a helpless thing.

And the patriotism is there, the dirge for heroes giving all for their country, sounded by one whose heart knew what they gave, knew well what they gave, and what they gave it for — America, sung by this man as never yet by anyone else, in verses that must live as long as the nation lasts, that must live until even America comes to understand them — America, with its immensity, its fertility, its multiplicity, its turbulence, its vast problems and its vaster hope.

It is by love and by hope chiefly that these poems exist. No one has poured out the hope of democracy with such joyous and infectious confidence. It may seem sometimes that the hope is willful, blind, over-looks immense and terrible dangers. Yet the per-ception of dangers is keen and present, if you look for it. The threat 'of the never-ending audacity of elected persons' is perfectly understood and the deepest tragedy of popular government has never been expressed better than in these words of pity:

As I stand aloof and look there is something to me profoundly
  affecting in large masses of men following the lead of
  those who do not believe in men.

But the confidence in democracy is justified be-cause it is not founded on mere claptrap and catchwords, but on the deepest sympathy with the human heart and the strongest sense of what democracy may be, must be, and some day will be. It is not the mere assertion of the ballot and of rights too often self-destructive and not good enough to fight for, but the vision of a whole society based on the large, rational enjoyment of those things that are best worth enjoying, the normal health of the well-nourished, well-disciplined, well-fostered body, the common magic of great art, the endlessly varied resources of natural beauty. In the latter especially Whitman finds depths of consolation, of charm, of unutterable rapture, certainly not surpassed in American poetry.

Jupiter shall emerge, be patient, watch again another night,
    the Pleiads shall emerge,
They are immortal, all those stars both silvery and golden
    shall shine out again,
The great stars and the little ones shall shine out again, they
    endure,
The vast, immortal suns and the long-enduring pensive moon
    shall again shine.

Above all, Whitman's democracy is solid and vital because it is based on God. Amiel's *Journal* begins, 'There is but one thing needful — to possess God.' Whitman declares, in words closely similar: 'For America, and for today, just the same as any day, the supreme and final science is the science of God — what we call science being only its minister — as Democracy is, or shall be also.' It is true that, for doctrine of God, *Leaves of Grass* wanders into strange places. It may be none the worse and none the less near God for that. It is true that the poet avoids all definitions, all dogmas, and in so doing is only the better poet and the wiser worshiper. But it is the sense of God that inspires his thought of man:

What do you suppose I would intimate to you in a hundred
    ways, but that man or woman is as good as God?
And that there is no God any more divine than yourself?

It is the sense of God that gives intensity even to the fullest life of the body. It is the sense of God that gives glow and splendor to trees and flowers and birds and clouds and stars. More than all, it is the sense of God that solves the greatest problem of life — death. Does not God vibrate in every syllable of that strange chant which salutes death in all its glory, in all its cloud of mystical possibilities beyond the sordid tumult of this world?

From me to thee glad serenades,
Dances for thee I propose saluting thee, adornments and
    feastings for thee,
And the sights of the open landscape and the high-spread sky
    are fitting,
And life and the fields, and the huge and thoughtful night.

But a simpler word than these yokes God and death together in a final verdict for the man, and for his view of life, and for his view of all our lives:

And I say to mankind, Be not curious about God,
For I who am curious about each am not curious about God,
(No array of terms can say how much I am at peace about
    God and death.)

IV
CHARLOTTE CUSHMAN

CHRONOLOGY

Charlotte Cushman
  Born, Boston, July 23, 1816.
  Appeared as a singer, at the Tremont Theatre, Boston, 1835, in *The Marriage of Figaro*.
  Entered the drama as Lady Macbeth, 1835.
  Undertook the management of the Walnut Street Theatre, Philadelphia, 1842.
  Accompanied Macready on his American tour of 1843.
  Début in London, 1845.
  Last appearance at the Globe Theatre, Boston, 1875.
  Died, Boston, February 18, 1876.

CHARLOTTE CUSHMAN

IV

CHARLOTTE CUSHMAN

I

WHEN the Pilgrims came to Plymouth in 1620, they brought with them the English conscience and intellect and energy, but, roughly speaking, it may be said that the English imagination stayed behind, with the children of Shakespeare. Now, humanity demands imagination as well as conscience, and it is most curious to trace in New England the gradual assertion of the imaginative type. Assuredly in Charlotte Cushman we have an interesting spectacle of the development of the two elements, not exactly in conflict, but in marked contrast, and existing side by side on the whole in well-balanced efficiency.

Miss Cushman was born in Boston in 1816. She belonged to the best New England stock on both sides of the family, and was brought up in comfortable surroundings and with an excellent education. Perhaps she would never have been attracted directly to the stage, though from her childhood she was remarkable as a mimic. Her early aspirations were musical, and she hoped that her powerful contralto voice might be developed to operatic quality. Her disappointment as to this was a bitter blow. but incidentally she had discovered that, though she could not sing, she could act, and she

97

continued to do so, with a career of mainly triumphant and unbroken success, until the cruel malady of cancer, which she bore with heroic patience, made it impossible for her to give even the dramatic readings in which she was quite as effective as on the actual stage. She died in 1876.

It may be said at once that Miss Cushman's life was one of full, joyous, and complete absorption in her work and devotion to it. She had no apologies for her profession, no distrust of it, no shame about it. On the contrary, she fully believed that it was one of the highest means of spiritual development and education for humanity, and that while the theatrical art might often have been degraded, it really represented a lofty mission of usefulness and the conscientious actor was justified in regarding himself as an important and honorable social instrument. It is hardly necessary to say that, with such a temper as hers, this view meant constant devotion and sacrifice. Her work was never trifling, never frivolous, she never slighted it or neglected it. Her soul was in whatever she did, and her biographer justly says, 'If I were asked what special quality distinguished her then, and indeed throughout her whole life, my reply would be, intensity.' Or, as Miss Cushman herself more vividly expresses it: 'To be thoroughly *in earnest*, intensely in earnest in all my thoughts and in all my actions, whether *in* my profession or *out* of it, became my one single idea. And I honestly believe herein lies the secret of my success in life.'

This affection, this passion, for her art made her ready to overlook all the drawbacks and annoyances which repel so many from the theatrical life who might otherwise succeed in it. How different is the attitude of Macready, who toiled at his profession with enormous patience, yet all the time despised it, and prayed that his children might not inherit any taste for 'this worst exercise of a man's intellect'; or, again, 'the wretched art which I have been wasting my life upon.' To Miss Cushman it was a noble art, and required all a man's energy and genius to make and keep himself worthy of it. Even the humbler and the harsher sides of it she valued as a useful spiritual discipline, and in one curious passage she relates how she made use of the discipline to purify and elevate her spirit when it was worn and shattered with some special strain and misery: 'It became necessary that I should suffer *bodily* to cure my heart-bleed. I placed myself professionally where I found and knew all my mortifications in my profession, which seemed for the time to strew ashes over the loss of my child-brother (for he was my child, and loved me best in all the world), thus conquering my art, which, God knows, has never failed me — never failed to bring me rich reward — never failed to bring me comfort.' And she sums up this beneficent element of her work in one effective sentence, 'Art is an exacting mistress, but she repays with royal munificence.'

In Miss Cushman's case, as in that of any imaginative artist, back of the intense immediate enjoyment of artistic effort and achievement, there was the long, conscious ambition to succeed, to make a great place in the world, to leave a great name behind her. And no doubt, in thoughtful moments she was clearly conscious of the defective side of this ambition, so far as the stage is concerned. No art is capable of such immediate, intense, directly appreciated triumph. And no other art is so ephemeral in its appeal, leaves so little permanent impress on the imagination of humanity. Miss Cushman saw this perfectly well, and deplored it: 'What is or can be the record of an actress, however famous? They leave nothing behind them but the vaguest of memories.... Other artists — poets, painters, sculptors, musicians — produce something which lives after them and enshrines their memories in positive evidences of their divine mission; but we — we strut and fret our hour upon the stage, and then the curtain falls and all is darkness and silence.' Yet, after all, there is something to be said for the glory which comes in one's lifetime, if it ever comes, and the immense, immediate applause of thousands laughing and weeping right before you may be worth a good deal more than the shadowy adoration of a dream-posterity. At any rate, there can be no doubt that ambition, the desire to achieve glory, if possible, and as much of it as possible, was a substantial, enduring motive in Miss Cushman's life. One little sentence is enough to show it, to prove conclusively how she reached outward and upward always to greater and greater things: 'I bless my mother for one element in my nature, or rather my grandmother — *ambition*. I cannot endure the society of people who are beneath me in character or ability. I hate to have satellites of an inferior calibre.'

And if glory was what she sought, she certainly got it, in large measure and perhaps as little mixed as often falls to the lot of anyone in this complicated world. So far as one can judge of her acting from the varied comments of critics, it was, as one might expect, perhaps stronger in the intellectual than in the impassioned aspect. She had a mighty and ardently impetuous temperament, and no doubt she lost herself in the emotional sway of her creations to a very great extent. Still, the main impression seems to be one rather of profound, penetrative intellectual power than of immediate, spontaneous self-abandonment, as for example with Salvini. She was universally recognized as a very great actress, but perhaps rather of the Saxon than of the Latin type.

In consequence, her successes and triumphs may not always have been so violent and sensational as in some cases, but her hold on the intelligent portion of her audiences was sure and lasting. In America everywhere and in Europe her reputation grew, and she was received with admiration and enthusiasm, not only in the lesser parts, like Meg Merrilies, which she had created and which died

with her, but in the great Shakespearean characters, which can never die, and which each actress
re-creates for herself. Perhaps the hints of what
her glory was are best caught in her own reflections
of it, the hasty accounts of triumphant receptions
which she scribbles off to her family and friends.
Thus, in early days, we hear of the 'particulars of
my great and triumphant success of last night, of
my reception, of being called out after the play,
and hats and handkerchiefs waved to me, flowers
sent to me, etc.' And it was just the same to the
end: 'When I got into my carriage at the private
entrance, expecting to go quietly to the hotel,...
I found myself surrounded by a mass of human
beings with torches and fireworks, rockets sent up
all the way along up to the front entrance of the
hotel, and a most indescribable noise and confusion.... I was ready to drop with fatigue, so I only
could wave my handkerchief to them, and went in,
not getting to my bed before half-past two.'

And of course it all delighted her, the hand-
clapping, the shouting, the fireworks, and the
general ecstasy. It was the seal of reward for
a life of prolonged and noble effort, and she enjoyed
it, and what human being would not? She naturally missed it, when by any accident it failed to
come, and the lack made her uneasy and restless, as
is indicated in the letter to Mrs. Fields, suggesting
that her husband might arouse a little enthusiasm
in the newspapers. But generally there was no
lack, rather a superabundance, amounting almost

to surfeit, if anyone could be surfeited with nourishment of that kind. That Miss Cushman's appetite for it was as wide and lasting as most appears in the pretty anecdote of her behavior on one conspicuous occasion when she had been for some time absent from the stage: 'Just then the storm of applause burst out afresh for a second "call"; as Miss Cushman heard it, she threw up her arms with a peculiar gesture, and cried out in a tone of indescribable, passionate, eager ecstasy: "Oh! how have I lived without this through all these years!"'

It is very obvious that no such career could pass without its drawbacks, its struggles and trials, and its bitterness. There were the critics always. Sometimes they said harsh things from mere prejudice, from conventional association, or favoritism for others. If the actor gets many kind words, when he is successful, he is bound also to get plenty of cruel ones, and they hurt, perhaps all the more, when you feel that they are not deserved. Then, even the greatest artists make mistakes, set their hearts passionately upon what they are unfitted for, and get just the same rebuff from an unfeeling world that comes to those who have no genius whatever. Something of this Miss Cushman found at the very start, when she failed in her musical career. The drama was not what she wanted; she wanted to be a great singer, and she couldn't, though she believed she could, and the disappointment stung. Again, like all actors, she would try parts for which nature had not intended her. Her somewhat masculine stature and carriage made her sometimes inclined to play young heroes. Her Hamlet was one of her favorites, though I do not know that others thought so much of it. Listen to Wagner's account of her attempt in later years to play Romeo, of his surprise 'at their giving the part of Romeo to an old man, whose age must at least be sixty, and who seemed anxious to retrieve his long-lost youth by laboriously adopting a sickly-sweet feminine air.'

The best and greatest are never quite free from such attempts and such failures and such disappointments as these. But perhaps even worse than the concrete individual failure is the general sense of disillusion, the days of discouragement when the high rapture of the taut nerves leaves you, and it seems as if your best effort and your longest struggle could never reach their aim, if indeed the aim is worth reaching. It was this kind of discouragement which, in part at least, accounted for the various decisions to retire, so much criticized in Charlotte as in others of her profession. Even if you are a very great actress, you see someone who seems to you greater, and the sun suddenly drops out of heaven, as when Charlotte writes of Rachel: 'Often, as I left the theatre, and compared my own acting with hers, despair took possession of me, and a mad impulse to end life and effort together.' Or some trifle makes you realize that popular favor is won by tricks and held by compromises, and that the serious study and passion of the artist are too often thrown away, as Charlotte remarked bitterly in regard to Meg Merrilies, 'with an outlandish dress and a trick or two, I can bring much more money to the theatre than when I give the public my heart's blood in my finest characters.' When you have the artistic temperament, that temperament which the Pilgrims forgot to bring over, these things depress as much as the high praise exalts, and Miss Cushman had that temperament in splendid fullness.

II

It shows not only in connection with her professional life, but in all the aspects of her career and character. She threw herself with her whole soul into what she was doing. If she succeeded, if things went well and as she wished, she was elevated to the clouds. When they went wrong, the depression was equally immediate and immense, as she said on one occasion, letting her head fall on the shoulder of a friend, 'Oh, I am dead and buried.' The force of impulse in her was enormous, sometimes erratic and surprising, but often leading to great and permanent results, 'knowing the sort of intense animal I am,' she writes to a friend, and her friends did know it, and she was.

So the intensity which she threw into creation went also into passive enjoyment. Take the great poets: she read them effectively, because she loved them and felt them first herself. Take her ecstasy over the poetry of Tennyson, which flowed perhaps as superbly from her lips as from his: 'Never was such a master of versification in our time. *The Lady of Shalott*, read in a *measure* slowly, is like a gentle flowing river, "as it goes down to Camelot"!' In the same way she vibrated to the subtle and varied rhythms of Shakespeare, and so made others vibrate as she did.

Again, music was always a delight to her, and with this, as with everything, her first instinct was to communicate her delight. Up to her last years she was fond of singing in companies of friends. The effort was not always appreciated, as witness the comment of Story, who, to be sure, was not particularly well-disposed: 'The Cushman sings ballads in a hoarse, manny voice, and requests people recitatively to forget her not. I'm sure I shall not.' At any rate, she tried to give what was given to her. As always, the intense personal interest predominated, in the feeling for art, as in everything else. Her friends were sculptors; therefore she had a passionate interest in sculpture. Beauty of all sorts appealed to her, but the art that was personally hers seemed to her in the end to include and involve all the rest: 'No one knows better than myself, after all my association with artists of sculpture or painting, how truly *my* art comprehends all the others and surpasses them, in so far as the study of mind is more than matter.'

And this intensely personal quality, of course, made her and kept her always a social being. She liked men and women about her, to feel them and touch them and enter into their lives and have them enter into hers. Like all thoughtful people, she knew the value of being alone. One who knew her well says that her spirit 'dwelt apart, in its loneliness, as well of suffering that no one could share as of an imaginative life that no one could fathom.' Like all busy people, she appreciated the pest of superficial visiting, 'receiving of visits — which are the moths of life, I think.' But in the main she was ready for human faces, liked to put smiles into them, and knew that, to do so, you must have smiles on your own, and in your heart. 'She had a real genius for enjoyment,' says her biographer, and there is no richer gift for social success. She herself declared that social life was necessary to her, that it was vain to try under any circumstances to seclude her from the warm contact of mortality: 'I am sympathetic, and so more a lover of my kind than most people; hence I must *see* people, and it is useless to attempt to box me up. I cannot be saved in this respect, and it is folly to try.'

It does not appear that she was in general especially brilliant or witty as a talker, but she always said what she thought with singular frankness and point, and this goes a good way. Joseph Jefferson, who was an excellent judge, praises her conversation highly: 'She had great tact in society, being perfectly at ease and making everyone else so. Her faculty for either entertaining or being entertained was remarkable. She could do all the listening or all the talking, whichever was the most agreeable to her guest.' And this gift of mutual response is as rare as it is valuable.

There is a ravishing variation of testimony as to Miss Cushman's social manner, so great that it is difficult to reconcile everything, though perhaps one may contrive it by suggesting that she was by nature and by profession an actress, and when she was most herself there was always something of the actress about her. The most bitter of her critics, W. J. Stillman, of whom more later, insists that 'she never lost sight of the footlights, and the best acting I ever saw her in was in private and in the representation of some comedy or tragedy of her own interests.' Mrs. Fields, who was not bitter at all, says quietly: 'She is a woman of effects. She lives for effect, and yet doing always good things and possessed of most admirable qualities.' On the other hand, Miss Stebbins, who lived with her intimately for years, and perhaps got to feel the effects as a second nature, writes: 'Not that, like Garrick "when off the stage always acting"; far from it: off the stage she was invariably — as she cordially expressed it in Julia in *The Hunchback* — "her open, honest, independent self."'

At any rate, however she managed, it is evident that she impressed people, attracted people, charmed some people, and always kept people about her. Perhaps the quality of her general social relation, its wide range and at the same time firm personal grasp, is well summed up in her own ample phrase: 'She used to say, "This is Liberty Hall; everyone does as *I* please."'

In the more intimate ties the same intense personal feeling appears even more vividly. Miss Cushman's attachment and devotion to the members of her family were always unfailing. Her relations were the objects of her constant thought and care. How much experience she herself had of love-making is not directly shown to us; but there are interesting stories about it. When she was a music-student in Boston, working hard at her art, but personally solitary, she became engaged to a young man of excellent family, who seems to have been ardently devoted to her. The engagement lasted some time, and Charlotte even visited the young man's mother in the country, as to which visit odd and characteristic anecdotes are told. Charlotte came driving up one afternoon on the outside of the stage, in animated conversation with two young men. Her prospective mother-in-law, who had never seen her, received her cordially, and congratulated her on having found acquaintances. 'Acquaintances?' laughed Charlotte. 'I never saw them before, but I am going to ride with one of them tomorrow.' So next morning the youth appeared, leading an extra horse. Charlotte mounted, galloped off at once, and returned in an hour or so, laughing gayly, having kept about a half-mile ahead of her companion all the way. It may well be imagined that a week of diversions like this did not wholly predispose a staid New England matron

in her future daughter-in-law's favor. Perhaps the
experience did not augur very well for Charlotte's
happiness. Perhaps she felt so herself. At any
rate, when it came to an absolute choice between
her lover and her career, the lover was discarded —
with much or little anguish, who shall say? Possibly a passage in her later letters refers to this
struggle: 'There was a time in my life of girlhood,
when I thought I had been called upon to bear the
very hardest thing that can come to a woman.
A very short time served to show me, in the harder
battle of life which was before me, that this had
been but a spring storm, which was simply to help
me to a clearer, better, richer, and more productive
summer.' Very shortly after the lover died.

There is no sign of any later thought of marriage
in Miss Cushman's career, or even of any distinct
approach to attachment, so far as men were concerned. Her life was full, however, of ardent devotion to women friends, who worshiped her and
were worshiped by her. This was true of women
of her own age and her own position, women who
would not have flattered her or anyone. Mrs.
Carlyle, for instance, was no hero-worshiper, or
runner after celebrities, and she wrote to Charlotte:
'I do wish to see you; do wish to hear from you, do
love you.... And further, I mean deliberatively
and imperatively that we two should be friends for
the rest of our lives.' But, besides these distinguished relations, Miss Cushman had a group of
younger followers to whom she devoted her life

with a self-forgetting ardor. 'Everything I do in this world I do *hard*,' she says, 'even to loving my friends.' How intense and how complete the surrender was is well shown by one charming passage of self-confession: 'Unless I can utterly forget myself, I am as nothing; and this is why you care for me, why my own friends love and judge me kindly; because, when I can talk freely upon the subjects which interest and occupy me, without a thought of myself or the impression I am making, all is well enough, and my life, my character through my life, makes itself *felt*.'

It is indeed possible that this extreme zeal of friendship sometimes led Miss Cushman to overlook other obligations and rights. W. J. Stillman, to whom I have already referred and who knew her well in Rome and elsewhere, insists that this disregard was excessive and scandalous. He urges that, for the sake of advancing the interests of the sculptors who were intimate with her personally, she was ready to undermine the reputation and injure the business of all the other American artists. According to Stillman, Miss Cushman's prejudices were so strong and her passions so ardent, as to blind her to all considerations of courtesy or even decency. Those about her must bow to her sway, accept her domination, advance her objects, or be swept from her path. There is little evidence besides Stillman's to support this extreme view, and I should not even refer to it if the man did not show himself generally to be a shrewd and careful judge of character and widely conversant with human life. His analysis of Charlotte is so fiercely adverse that one can regard it only as the manifestation of contrast and conflict between two temperaments alike in energy and salience but differing totally in their general attitude toward life.

At the same time, it must be admitted that a milder glimpse of what Stillman means is afforded also by the remark of Mrs. Fields that 'it is amusing to see how full her letters are of suggestions for forwarding her own plans or those of others in whom she was interested.' In other words, the woman lived with passion, her soul was absorbed with fierce intensity by whatever happened to appeal to her at the moment, and minor considerations, even of others' comfort or convenience, were overlooked. In this aspect she was all life, all fire, a creature of ample and magnificent temperament.

III

Yet the solid substructure of New England character and intelligence was there all the time, sometimes reënforcing the temperament, sometimes checking it. You can see the sterner elements in the face and figure. There was no feminine charm, no grace, or witching tenderness, and it is said that Miss Cushman sometimes longed for these things with a profound longing. 'I would rather be a pretty woman than anything else in this world.' Instead, there was a deep, resonant, immensely varied and penetrating, but always slightly masculine voice, firm, substantial, strongly marked features, and a commanding presence, which impressed and imposed, but hardly fascinated. Her dress suited her face: it was always neat and well chosen, but not coquettish or extreme in fashion. And the character showed in far other things than the face. There was the capacity for work. After all, genius in any line gets so little way without the habit of industry behind it. One who knew Miss Cushman well says of her: 'Higher than her intellectual strength, higher than her culture or genius or graces of character, she ranked her ability for *work*.' When a task had to be done, she threw herself into it, no matter how distasteful it was, or how weary she was, and it was done. Even, she knew well the curative, the mere spiritual value of labor for itself, independent of the object. In one period of stress and trial she frankly declares: 'I conquered my grief and myself. *Labor* saved me then and always, and so I proved the eternal goodness of God.' At the same time she was not wasteful of her energies. They were always husbanded, and thoughtfully directed; for none knew better than she that, work as we may, and struggle as we may, there is always far more left to accomplish than one life will suffice to achieve.

In some of these aspects of work and the intelligent and frugal guidance of it, as in so many phases of her character, there is the undeniable suggestion of something masculine. And there was a virile element in her, which she strove neither to diminish nor conceal. She herself says, 'I was born a tomboy,' and all her life she liked active and even dangerous sports and amusements. She was passionately fond of riding, as appears in the anecdote I have already quoted as to her youthful love-affair. She liked animals, and was tenderly devoted to them, but especially to her horses. During the years she spent in Rome, fox-hunting in the Campagna was a favorite occupation with her, and Mr. Lodge gives an interesting account of her engagement in this pursuit: 'She was a very large, heavy woman, over fifty years of age then, and she rode carefully, but she also rode well and intelligently, and she was perfectly mounted, kept up and saw all that was going on.'

Whether, in the intervals of sighing for female loveliness, Charlotte ever sighed for a complete transference to the other sex, I cannot say. But I doubt it. To be sure, she liked to play male parts. But I imagine she was well aware that masculine energy and feminine privileges make a very successful and effective combination in the practical affairs of life. At any rate, she manifested that combination in a wonderful aptitude for business. Her early years had been passed in a more or less constant struggle with narrow means, and in consequence she had always a keen sense of the value of money and a wide appreciation of the desirability and the varied methods of obtaining it. This prominence of the financial side is undeniably a rather ungracious element in her. There was no deprecation of profit, no retiring eschewal of the imputation of active acquisitiveness. She wanted a lot of money, to use in broad and generous ways and for good purposes, but she wanted it, and she got it. In her early years she wrote begging a loan to go to Europe: 'It would be doing me a charity to put me in the way of future affluence.' At a later period she looked over with a sigh at the money that was being made at home: 'I hear you are making your fortune. Alas, why am not I? If Emma had only been content to stop in America this year, I would have made mine too, but she would not, and I sit here and groan.'

It was not her habit to entrust business affairs to others, or to let the artist's delicacy keep her out of the hot struggle of dollars and cents. It is true that she sometimes complained of the difficulty of working alone: 'I have nobody to trust in money matters.' The world was hard and bitter to contend with: 'He is a tricky old manager and I am a fool, so we are not equally matched.' But she preferred to work alone, and I am not sure she did not enjoy it. She liked to fight, she liked to drive a close bargain and get the best of it, she liked to win and dominate and control.

To Stillman it appeared that this desire to dominate amounted to cruelty and unscrupulousness. Miss Stebbins, who knew her friend far more intimately, but was perhaps also somewhat prejudiced, puts the point in a very different form:

'What was right she would have, and she knew how to bend the most stubborn materials to her behests; and yet this was never done in a domineering or captious spirit, but by the sheer force of "character," that most supreme of gifts.' The right is probably with Miss Stebbins; but it is evident that Miss Cushman had her way, and was determined to have it, and while there is no proof that she was substantially unjust or unreasonable or unpopular, I doubt if those who came under her management had always a very good time of it.

In all these matters Miss Cushman showed her clear, energetic, penetrating New England intelligence. Her temperament might absorb her, inflame her; it did not fool her. Her brain was vigorous, active, and unclouded: it went straight to the heart of life, whether as reflected in the great dramas that she studied professionally, or as embodied in the flesh and blood creatures that she saw about her. Take the following superb analysis and portrayal of Mrs. Carlyle: 'Clever, witty, calm, cool, unsmiling, unsparing, a *raconteur* unparalleled, a manner *un*imitable, a behavior scrupulous, and a power invincible — a combination rare and strange exists in that plain, keen, unattractive, yet unescapable woman.' In some respects this sketch would almost seem to serve for Charlotte herself, and it is easy to see how, in the direct, concrete management of life, men and women and facts yielded to her, because she applied her profound intellectual power to mould them as she wished.

CHARLOTTE CUSHMAN

IV

Once again to revert to the bitter criticism of Stillman, who was so deeply impressed by this intellectual power that it appeared to him to crowd out all moral qualities entirely: 'I think she possessed an utterly selfish nature, was not at all scrupulous in the attainment of her purposes, and was, in effect, that most dangerous member of society, a strong-willed and large-brained woman without a vestige of principle.' It is interesting to see this impression produced upon an acute, and on the whole generally fair-minded, observer by the striking prominence of certain undeniable and even admirable qualities in Miss Cushman, while he remains oblivious of other qualities, which are equally undeniable, indisputable, not only from the testimony of her friends, but from the far more substantial testimony of her own actions and written words. The presence of the New England conscience in her is just as clear as that of the New England brain, and her great moral qualities were as persistent and as impressive as the mental.

Her eminent and unfailing loyalty is denied by no one; indeed, in its exaggerated form it makes the basis of the charges against her. With all her subtlety and suppleness, she had a singular large simplicity of nature, a frankness and abandon of candor, which are so often characteristic of New England at its best. And there was, too, a fundamental goodness about her, a quick response to

what was high and fine in life and thought, which
may have been at times obscured by prejudice or
the ardor of success, but which shone out at its
best when she was quiet and untroubled. William
Winter even says that her genius 'was saturated
with goodness,' which may serve as an antidote
to Stillman's diatribes.

Or, to look at the various elements of this moral
nature more concretely: Take business. For all
her zest for success, her keen scent for money and
acquisition, she was highly honorable, would not
condescend to a mean or dubious action. Her word
once passed must be kept, whatever the conse-
quences to herself. 'I have just returned from the
theatre, after acting the new play for the second
time. It has not succeeded; but my word was
pledged to do it, and I have kept my word.' Obligations of all kinds must be met, whatever the
cost. This was true of the social and the financial
both. 'Sometimes my friends argue with me on
what they consider the wrong of yielding to all the
social claims made upon me; but I have an innate
necessity for repaying an obligation.' Also, I like
much the simple sentence in the midst of one of
her hard, practical, pointed business letters: 'I did
not want to lose money.' She did not want to lose
money herself, and she certainly did not want
others to lose it by her means.

Take again, professional jealousy. This is,
rightly or wrongly, supposed to be peculiarly characteristic of those who seek prominence upon the

stage, perhaps because jarring pretensions and efforts are brought so much more closely into contact and juxtaposition before the footlights than elsewhere. Even her critics do not accuse Miss Cushman of being narrow or mean in this respect. It is true that she quarreled with Forrest, as pretty much everybody did. Forrest was an easy man to quarrel with; witness Jefferson's account of him and that of many others. He charged Miss Cushman with conspiring to discredit him, and she was naturally indignant and cherished some grudge. Yet, as Mrs. Clement wisely suggests, they probably respected each other in their hearts, the more so as there was a good deal of resemblance between their styles and their characters. How pretty is the story of the autograph-hunter who pursued both of them! 'Go first to Forrest,' said Miss Cushman: 'I cannot take precedence of so great a man.' Whereupon the collector had recourse to Forrest and received a similar reply. I wonder if he got his autographs. And in the main it is clear that Miss Cushman was largely sympathetic, or at least tolerant, with her competitors, and appreciated that the world had room for other styles and other glories besides her own.

She was not only tolerant, she was generous and helpful. Both in her profession and out of it, she was quick to see and feel the needs and troubles of others and to respond to and relieve them. She was ready to do this with money, according to her abilities and sometimes even beyond them. In this regard it is indeed interesting to see the constant presence of New England thrift and canniness. She had lived for years with little money herself. She knew that others could live with little, and she did not propose to be the prey of thoughtless extravagance and shiftlessness. When she was too urgently appealed to for local charities, she rebelled, and insisted that she gave in her own fashion and to her own people what she thought was right and did not intend to be bullied into throwing her earnings away for mere ostentation. She knew the value of pennies, none better, and her care in regard to them sometimes brought upon her the reputation of actual meanness. Yet no one gave more aptly, when there was real need, and especially gave more intelligently.

She gave her woman's heart, too, her sympathy and gentle, helpful comprehension. She well knew how often mere listening and listening rightly is the best help. A pretty story is told of one of her innumerable railroad journeys, when a woman sitting opposite her, after looking at her long and earnestly, asked if she might speak to her, and on receiving a cordial reply, confided the whole pitiful story of her life, to which Charlotte listened with absorbed interest and responded with appropriate advice. Something in her thoughtful, earnest, kindly face drew such confidences. Again, she could put herself in others' places, could gauge and understand their suffering by her own. One evening she was dressing hurriedly for a ball. A woman began to sing in the street below her window. Miss Cushman stopped her dressing and dispatched her faithful attendant, Sally, who shared all her experiences and perhaps more of her life than anyone else, to give the woman a substantial charity: 'I never hear a woman sing like that,' she said, 'but I think I might have been doing it myself.'

What is perhaps most curious of all in the spiritual side of Miss Cushman's life is the actual and constant presence of religious thinking and feeling. This does not seem to take any very definite form of creed or church affiliation. She may not have been particularly orthodox in her belief or in her practice. But the thought of God and the consideration of God, the reference of all daily interests and actions to God, seem to have been a powerful element in her make-up, and the analysis of this in her letters is exceedingly significant and interesting, making one almost think at moments of Emily Dickinson's preoccupation with similar topics.

As to actual belief in God, Miss Cushman constantly affirms it, not perhaps with any precise metaphysical definition, but with the glow of emotion which goes further than any metaphysics. 'Every human being who goes to sleep awakes believing in God, whatever he may call it.' Again: 'Trust me, every human being believes in a God. For me, I believe in all things good coming from God, in all forms, in all ways; my faith is firm in Him and His love. I believe in instincts marvellously. I doubt any power to take from me the love of God.'

Also, she did not for one moment regard her special occupation as in any way distracting or detached from this interest in God and love of Him. There are times, indeed, as with everyone, when it seems to her that she is not doing enough, or not what she should. 'But that God is perfect, and that my love for Him is without fear, I should be troubled in the thought that I am not doing all I should, *in this* sphere, to make myself worthy of happiness in the next.' But in the main she was convinced that, in doing her work in the world in the highest and best and most faithful manner she was capable of, she was doing God's work, and doing it as He would have it done. 'For I know He does not fail to *set* me His work to do, and helps me to do it, and helps others to help *me*. (Do you see this tracing back, and then forward, to an eternity of good, and do you see how better and better one can become in recognizing one's self as a minister of the Almighty to faithfully carry out our part of His great plan according to our strength and ability?) Oh, believe we cannot live one moment for ourselves, one moment of selfish repining, and not be failing Him at that moment, hiding the God-spark in us, letting the flesh conquer the spirit, the evil dominate the good.'

So, it is undeniable that, in spite of the splendid vigor and aggressiveness of her ample personality, she did not live for herself alone, ever, was always on the lookout for larger ends, was alive to the deeper interests of humanity, worked for patriotism, interesting herself passionately in the great struggle of the Civil War, worked for benevolence, worked for education, worked for the broader, more intelligent life of man and woman everywhere. And in doing this she gave a splendid example of making the spirit conquer the flesh to the very end, for she fought one of the bitterest battles that man or woman can fight with disease, and fought it with courage, with energy, with cheerfulness, till even her superb resistance was utterly worn out by a strain which would have conquered anyone else long before.

v

All which somehow does not sound quite like the ordinary conception of the actress's character, suggesting, as it does, to many of us, a shallow emotionalism, a somewhat superficial vanity, and a way of taking life which, to say the least of it, does not imply any passionate preoccupation with spiritual things. It is unnecessary to point out how many admirable contradictions there have been and are to such a conception as this of the theatrical career. It must be admitted, also, that there were even in Miss Cushman hints and intimations of what the stage habit and influence can be. Nevertheless, she was a distinguished, a noble, an impressive figure, and would have been so in any calling in life. When you have realized fully how intense her artistic temperament was, how it absorbed and transported her, with what free and entire possession it tended to dominate her thoughts and all her soul, you appreciate how great was the energy of character which could at all times control and subdue this temperament, make it a servant and not a master, an agent to do great things intelligently, securely, and always for great purposes. She was royal and supreme as an artist, because she had firmly established dominion over her own spirit: 'Teach yourself quiet and repose in the time you are waiting. With half your strength I could bear to wait and labor with myself to conquer *fretting*. The greatest power in the world is shown in conquest over self.'

Yet I confess that I relish most, and even I think Charlotte herself would have relished, the brief epitaph of the Mount Auburn grave-digger, who might have turned up skulls in the cemetery of Elsinore, 'She was considerable of a woman, for a play-actress.'

V
WILLIAM MORRIS HUNT

CHRONOLOGY

WILLIAM MORRIS HUNT

Born, Brattleboro, Vermont, March 31, 1824.

At Harvard, 1840.

Studied in Paris under Couture and Millet, 1843–1854.

Returned to America, 1855.

Settled in Boston, 1862.

Many of his paintings and sketches destroyed in the Boston
fire of 1872.

Died by drowning, Isles of Shoals, September 8, 1879.

WILLIAM MORRIS HUNT
Self-Portrait

V

WILLIAM MORRIS HUNT *

I

WILLIAM MORRIS HUNT lived to interpret the world in line and color. He thought and spoke only of painting. But this was not because he limited life, but because he believed that man and God, and all they involve and imply, could be expressed in art and transfigured by the immortal radiance of beauty. He left some admirable pictures and strove to infuse a slight tincture of his imaginative enthusiasm into the struggling, groping, crass materialism of young American democracy.

Hunt was born in Brattleboro, Vermont, in 1824. He was educated mainly in painting and largely in Europe. His earlier work was done in France under the influence of Couture and then of Millet. He returned to America, painted for a time in Newport, where he was vividly described by Henry James, married and had sons and daughters, set up his studio in Boston in 1862, and from that time painted, taught, talked, thought, and lived with a splendid, furious ardor that infected and fascinated all who came into contact with him.

* Since this portrait was written, Miss Martha A. S. Shannon, in her *Boston Days of William Morris Hunt*, has given an excellent critical account of the painter and his work.

WILLIAM MORRIS HUNT

In 1878, he was commissioned to decorate the Assembly Chamber in the New Capitol at Albany. The work came as the supreme effort and passionate crown of his artistic life. He wore himself completely out upon it and after some months of utter prostration he died by drowning at the Isles of Shoals in September, 1879.

Those who are competent to judge regard Hunt's painting as an important achievement in the history of American art. The collection of his pictures gathered by his daughter in the Boston Museum of Fine Arts goes far to prove this. And the 'Bathers,' Hunt's best-known picture, the superb portrait of Chief Justice Shaw at Salem, and the ample, lofty, impetuous 'Chariot of Night' in the Albany decorations will suffice to suggest the richness and variety of his work. His spirit, his fire, his distinction, his sensibility, are questioned by none. Some critics, however, feel that in his ardor to fix his dreams there was a neglect of finish, of perfect workmanship. And there is general agreement that there was more in the man than he was ever able fully to express. No doubt this is true of all artists; but it seems peculiarly true here, and the curious lack of individuality in Hunt's work, taken as a whole, the rapid passage from one style to another, and even blending of different styles in the same period, would seem to suggest one who was toiling with intense endeavor to find his way and did not quite succeed.

But my interest is more in the painter than in

the painting. Few men have interwoven their art
more completely with their lives and fewer have accompanied the constant progress of their art with
such brilliant and illuminating comment to help us
to elucidate both life and art. He saw pictures in
everything, beauty in everything, light in everything, or, if anything lacked light, he made light fall
upon it. 'I did not see the picture in nature, as we
walked together, till it was shown by him,' says
one of his friends. Not that he was pedantic, or
mechanical, always trying to force life into a frame.
He let beauty come to him with a sweet, idle largeness. 'If I am *looking*, I don't *see!* You must be
lazy, and say, "Let me see a thing, and I'll paint
it."' He had the whims and fantastic impulses of
genius. 'Essentially a painter of moods, and of
very violent moods, he subordinated everything to
the one idea that urged him to action. His work
was therefore uneven and uncertain. A trifle would
spoil it, an hour of satisfactory painting would
secure its completion.'

This does not mean that he was not a worker,
could not toil with the intense, terrible rapture
which is the highest delight that comes to the creative artist. He wanted no other occupation, no
diversion, no distraction, just to paint and paint
inexhaustibly. 'His actual product was enormous,
both in color and in black and white,' said Sarah
W. Whitman. 'Day after day, year after year, he
lived for and with his brush, endeavoring to turn
the confused chaos of the visible world into definite

revelations of artistic beauty.' And however there might be speed and fire in the close, there was the sense of the need of unavoidable labor at the bottom, the appreciation of the value and significance of minute detail. 'It is worth while to have done one thing as well as we know how; that is, to have made a careful study of an object for the sake of seeing how a *little* thing adds.'

Did he never tire, then? Oh, yes, he tired, like the rest of us. There were times of immense fatigue, but he knew in general how to meet them. 'He knew when to stop work — how to keep his mind free from that fatigue which ruins many a picture. When weariness was half suspected, he would lay down his brushes, close the studio, and go off for a drive.' And the wholesome fatigue of uninterrupted toil was much more bearable than the pin-pricks of illegitimate annoyance. Thus, during the last great work at Albany he writes: 'It's fatiguing, of course; but it's the things which bore you that kill you, not the fatiguing ones, and I'm never bored here at all. It don't take the life out of me half as much as thinking whether the family would like her eyes blue or not in a portrait!'

Also, though he could toil infinitely, he knew well that it is the direction of toil that counts, not its intensity, and that a clear brain and a heart of fire will do more in a day than an unlightened spirit in a month. Thus he did not hesitate to mock mere labor without intelligence: 'Look at what a critic says of some noodles, "At any rate, they have this in common with the old masters — persistent labor!" *So has a jackass!'* And he knew well the importance of choosing the heavenly moment to do a thing at once and do it swiftly. 'Oh, this is a funny old world; and how we dawdle and fool at nine o'clock in the morning, when we think we have time enough! At five P.M. we desire nothing so much as to paint.'

The driving motive at the back of all the labor was, of course, as with every artist, a healthy ambition to succeed, to do great things and win great glory. After all, however much we may resent and deplore it, the final word in all lines of life is that of General Albert Sidney Johnston: 'The test of merit in my profession, with the people, is success; it is a hard rule, but I think it right.' Doubtless there are different kinds of success, and some artists even assert that they find their own approbation enough. But the larger number prefer something a little more solid. It can never be said that Hunt sought a trivial or ostentatious notoriety. He did not cater to the taste of the day or try to please shallow critics with catchy flamboyance. He emphasized and re-emphasized to his pupils the danger of thinking too much of immediate success. It was almost as great as the danger of being over-scrupulous. 'Nothing like ambition to multiply lights. Conscientiousness and ambition play the Nick with pictures.' And he insisted on the importance of working for delight rather than for accomplishment: *'Paint for fun!* I don't care whether

131

it succeeds or not! Let success come along afterwards!' Yet no one has stated more vividly and succinctly the underlying passion or made more evident how greatly it inspired his own tumultuous soul. 'You mustn't be so ambitious,' he said to one pupil. And the pupil remonstrated, 'How can I help it?' And Hunt replied quietly, 'You can't.'

As regards what is generally considered the concrete test of artistic success in America, money-reward, Hunt was rather indifferent, perhaps partly because private means assisted him to be so. He enthusiastically favored the liberal expenditure of public funds for the creation of beauty: 'If the people's money had not been expended, there would have been no Acropolis, or anything else worth having; and I would like to know what expenditures have paid better.' But he deplored the tendency to commercialize the creative impulse and the disastrous effect upon genius of the constant attempt to try it by the financial standard: 'I might have painted if I had lived in an atmosphere of art, but in America everything resolves itself into the getting of money, and selling a poor article instead of a good one.' And more concisely: 'We cannot have two passions. No painter can paint and love money.'

In spite of these protests, Hunt, like most of his great predecessors and successors, was drawn by practical business considerations into the painting of portraits. Men and women will pay for making themselves conspicuous, when they will not pay for anything else, and if it were not for this general human weakness, it is difficult to see how art could live. Unfórtunately, when people pay, they expect to be pleased, and what pleases the artist does not always please the sitter. Hence arise untold tribulation, concessions, compromises, flatteries, insincerity, and in too many cases a result which is neither good art nor good portraiture and which dissatisfies the purchaser and embitters the painter. The history of portrait-painting would be indeed a history of the foibles and the weakness of the human heart. Hunt's position and habits, however, made him as little inclined to humor the whims of his patrons as any man ever was. If he was approached deferentially and with proper consideration, he was responsive. A lady asked him to paint her dead daughter from a photograph, described the child's temper and character and then said that she would leave the likeness entirely in his hands and accept the result. He was charmed, that was the way to treat an artist, who should not be dictated to, any more than a preacher should be dictated to about his sermons. And he painted the picture at once. But he had no patience whatever with the type of sitter who thinks that his money entitles him to respect, who feels that the distinction of painting him is a financial asset which should enter largely into the bargain. Such persons got no satisfaction out of William Hunt. Nor was it of any use to hint or nag or comment or suggest. His way of doing the thing, of seeing the thing, might not be your way; but it was his way, and it did no good to ask him to change it, especially if he had no particular respect for your opinion. The son of a distinguished sitter came in to look at the portrait. 'Is father's shirt as soiled as that?' he said. 'I thought that he wore a white one.' 'My God!' cried Hunt. 'Isn't your father anything but a white shirt?'

The man, like some other geniuses, was sensitive to trifles, and if you ruffled him, or crossed him, or disturbed him, the divine impetus was gone, and the achievement spoiled. He did not like his subjects to be condescending or to pretend that they were yielding only to the urgency of friends. Emerson was careful to point out that he was painted because his family wished it, and Hunt confessed that this attitude destroyed all his enthusiasm. Holmes seemed chiefly anxious to know how few sittings would finish the job, and in consequence Hunt soon civilly got rid of him. 'I don't like persuaded sitters,' he said. 'I never could paint a cat if the cat had any scruples, religious, superstitious, or otherwise, about sitting.'

With such susceptibility and sensitiveness, it will readily be understood that Hunt's way was not always smooth and easy, that he had to meet serious obstacles and had his times of discouragement and even despair. These did not really shake his glorious perseverance or his determination to do the work for which God put him into the world. He had in the main a cheerful temperament and looked at the bright side of things. Above all, he was not a man to whine or complain of the little casual ills that happen to all of us. 'Scarcely a lisp concerning his share in the common troubles of mortal life reached the ears even of his intimate friends,' says one who knew him well.

Yet if you examine carefully the abundant records of Hunt's career and especially his own comments upon it, you will see what the troubles were and the struggles and the intricate complications that beset every path to success in this difficult world. There were external troubles, troubles of circumstance, troubles of surroundings, little frets and vexations, which seem avoidable, at any rate negligible, and are sometimes the hardest to neglect. 'Once the noise of rats so disturbed the painter that he felt forced to seek new quarters. Then his numerous stoves gave him such trouble that he could not work. A slight leak in the roof, on another occasion, had a similar effect.' There was physical weakness, especially in later years, crowding and hampering just when the demands and opportunities for accomplishment came thickest. Hunt faced this nobly, till it grew overwhelming. When a friend asked him how he did, he replied, 'I don't know, and I don't care. If I cared, I suppose that I should know.' But the torment was real, just the same.

There was the sense of isolation in an unfavorable atmosphere, criticism that clacked and chattered and could not comprehend, a great, ignorant public that demanded gross, crude satisfactions and slighted the subtle and the obscure, few sympathetic and understanding fellow workers to stimulate achievement by wholesome rivalry. Mrs. Fields gives a striking account of Hunt's picture of this situation: He 'launched into a sea of talk upon his own life as a painter; of his lonely position here without anyone to look up to in his art; his idea being misunderstood; of his determination not to paint cloth and cheeks, but the glory of age and the light of truth.'

Finally, most blighting of all, there are the inner struggles of the creating spirit, the inexplicable delays, debates, obstacles, the barrenness, the doubt of self, far worse than any doubt of any critic. This cannot be described more vividly than in Hunt's own words: 'I tell you, it's no joke to paint a portrait. I wonder that I am not more timid when I begin. I feel almost certain that I can do it. It seems very simple. I don't think of the time that is sure to come, when I almost despair; when the whole thing seems hopeless. Into the painting of every picture that is worth anything, there comes, sometime, this period of despair!'

What is charming about Hunt is the complete candor with which he always discussed these difficulties. He may not have complained, but he confessed. The humility with which he admitted his defeats is as perfect as the shrewdness with which he saw them. How winning is this little note to Fields: 'I have had a delightful day with your friend and I know he is a painter — why — because he likes what I do well and *hates* what I do that ain't worth —— —.' How admirable is his caution to his pupils: 'You're all in such a hurry to learn to paint. Why, I've been at it all my life, and I don't feel that I know anything. I'm not sure that I can go on with a single one of these portraits that I've begun.'

Yet, side by side with these recognitions of incompetence and failure, there is at times the splendid exultation that comes to every true artist, the sense of having, for once in his life, done something that is really worth while, and being proud of it. Who will not sympathize with the painter's ecstasy over a piece of work that he had done years before? 'Ha! I'd like to see the man who could do that again! I couldn't. By George! I tell you what, look at that little bit, the feller must have known he had done a good thing by the time that was finished.'

Above all, whether success comes or failure, there is the pure, inexhaustible, incomparable felicity of the work itself: 'Painting, only, is worth while'; and again, 'Queer old thing — painting is; but we would rather die doing it than live doing anything else.'

II

Yet, though painting was much, it was not quite all, and Hunt, like others, was a man as well as an artist. It is of profound interest to establish this general human basis and then relate it to the one absorbing passion. He was at all times alive to what went on about him, quick to observe, sensitive to feel, eager to record. When someone remarked that Allston was not identified with the time in which he lived, Hunt insisted that that was not true of himself, and he was right.

And he was practical, business-like, understood the daily necessities of life, and, when it was required, could subject himself to them in the most systematic manner. To be sure, he had his whims and fancies. He liked to buy diamonds, which is certainly not an economical habit. But in general his management of money was discreet and prudent. No man was more naturally sensitive to comfort and luxury; yet he could deny himself without a murmur: 'I hate conveniences. That's my pet economy. I don't generally have conveniences.' And he was largely liberal for the needs and the comfort of others. In the matter of a bargain he was shrewd, far-seeing, and self-controlled. When a house was offered him that he very much wanted, he was willing to pay a certain price for it, and not a dollar more. 'A man must have a limit, and wherever you put the limit there you must remain.' Not all artists, nor all men of business, have restraint enough to fix such a limit and stick to it.

As regards general education and thought, Hunt had the same shrewdness as in business matters. He was not widely conversant with books and was no great devotee of them. He did not complete his course at Harvard, having a mind much too wide open to other things to be concentrated upon humdrum studies, and all his life he was ready to take a fling at Cambridge and the academic atmosphere: 'Cambridge was like Kaulbach's pictures. It was all literature. There was nothing there to stimulate or develop the perceptions, and everything to suppress instinct and enthusiasm. One learned neither to see nor to feel.' Yet, like many people who read little, he seemed to know the best that books had in them. Above all, he remembered all that he read and all that he heard.

His interest in abstract subjects, politics and religion, was general, human, not concrete, or immediate, or dogmatic. When he met John Brown at a dinner, he was impressed because Brown refused oysters on the ground that he was not hungry: 'Did you ever know a man to refuse oysters at a party because he was not hungry?... Was not going to gorge himself — a man with such a destiny before him.' I think his attitude toward God was much like his attitude toward John Brown, admiration inspiring sympathy and tenderness. At any rate, his religion abhorred pretense, believed that good, honest work was the best worship and the most deserving of respect. 'So they objected to your painting on Sunday,' he said to a pupil. 'You might have told them that your work is one sort of prayer. It's good for nothing if it isn't. And it isn't "Now I lay me down to sleep," either.' Work was one sort of prayer, and another sort was the noble passage that closes his *Talks on Art*, words strangely prefiguring his own end in the quiet pool at the Isles of Shoals: 'I was thinking of this subject of Eternity the other night, when I looked at the moon, and saw, before it, a church-spire, a finger pointing upward into space. Next the spire, the moon. Beyond the moon a fixed star. Next — what? Eternity. A ripple closes over us.'

To beauty outside his own exquisite art, Hunt was always delicately susceptible. That the charm of nature appealed to him, haunted him, is sufficiently evident from his painting. He felt not only the broader splendor of the external world, but its subtler aspects, and had suggestive words for rendering them. His remark about pussy-willows has all the tender insight of Emily Dickinson: 'Those pussy-willows are hard things to paint. Their beauty is not general, but intimate.' His delight in music came early and endured and increased. He played on both violin and piano before he was fifteen, and his violin, once owned by Balzac, was a constant resource when the fatigue and strain of painting became unbearable. He made shrewd comments on both the performance of music and the enjoyment of it.

For the more superficial diversions of mankind, Hunt cared little. When friends urged him to seek amusement, he replied that his painting was all the amusement he required: 'For me it is the only work worth doing, and there is no other play.' Nevertheless, he was always fond of horses. When he was a student in Paris, he drove a tandem through the Latin Quarter. Henry James portrayed him vividly at Newport, as 'he passed in a spinning buggy, his beard flying, behind a favorite trotter.' At all times in his life a bargain in horses tempted him. He became attached to his horses individually; yet, like all collectors, he was always selling and exchanging, in the excitement of securing something new and untried. The fruit of his equine passion shows best in the magnificent coursers that sweep the chariot of Night through tumultuous skies, one of the largest and surest things that Hunt ever did.

But what most marks Hunt as truly and broadly human is his relations with other human beings. He was at all points alive, keenly and intensely interested in the sufferings and struggles and hopes of the men and women who moved about him. He was one day complaining of a man's work, but could not see what the fault was. 'He's cold-hearted,' suggested a friend. 'Yes, you have hit it! That's just the trouble.' No one could ever say that Hunt was cold-hearted, or his pictures. He could indeed sympathize with Whistler's irritation against the perpetual demand for 'a story': 'Most people will mix the dramatic with painting. They want a story in a picture, and will gape until you say, "That means so — and so." Then they are interested.' Yet he felt the natural human yearning under the demand and all his impulse was to comply with it.

His human sympathy was large, general, democratic. He felt the toil and struggle of the humbler masses. It was this which drew him to Millet and the French realists, who struck down into the deep, dumb, common sources of passion and life. Only he shrank instinctively from the pessimism of the French, liked light and hope and joy, and avoided and resented the gloomy, the ugly, and the coarse. But, whatever their occupation or their garb, he appreciated the people, real, substantial human beings — appreciated them, and tried to put them into his art. 'Do you see that old Irishman? He is the chap that I spoke to you about. I'll put him where he will "tell," for he has more character than an entire Congress. See how big his movement is. Doesn't he handle that hoe with the dignity of a king?'

And as his sympathy was broad, so it was also acute and personal. His heart leaped at once in pity for suffering, and his keen intelligence was apt and ingenious to relieve it. As he came down his studio stairs one morning, he found an old woman trying to carry out a barrel of ashes. Instantly he took hold and was soon seen depositing the ashes on the sidewalk. One day a forlorn organ-grinder came into the neighborhood. Hunt was touched, seized the organ himself, played it to his friends thereabout, and realized quite a sum of money for the astonished Italian. When he was staying at Niagara, his sister spoke of a sick child whom she had seen during the afternoon. 'I believe I can cure that child,' said Hunt, after hearing the story. It was late and dark and raining, but he went and did not return till one o'clock in the morning. 'How's your child?' he was asked. 'She's all right. I left her sleeping; and I tell you, that kind of work pays.'

The affection and tenderness which thus went out generally to humanity were naturally far more intense when concentrated upon sympathetic individuals. Hunt loved many people, loved them devotedly, discriminatingly, and helpfully, and was beloved by them in return. His broad, sunny, cheerful temperament turned to others with ever-ready kindliness and solicited an infinite response.

Above all, his natural element was society, the quick and eager converse of intelligent and understanding spirits. Like all persons who think and feel, he was capable of vast solitude, and could enrich it and profit by it. But he did not often seek it, liked to have men and women about him, to impart his thoughts and feelings, believed that they were quickened, doubled by such contact. He had a singular charm, an infectious gayety and good-humor, that inspired and stimulated people and made them feel at home, gave them an ease and even a sparkle which they did not commonly find in their homespun daily souls.

Something about his appearance, his unique aspect and bearing, accentuated the charm, and helped to make him prominent in any company. Read Henry James's account of him, as characteristic of James as of Hunt, 'all muscular spareness and brownness and absence of waste, all flagrant physiognomy, brave bony arch of handsome nose, upwardness of strong eyebrow and glare, almost, of eyes that both recognized and wondered, strained eyes that played over questions as if they were objects and objects as if they were questions.' And this odd physique leads James to trifle, in his shadowy manner, with the suggestion of a modern Don Quixote.

Certainly there was something Quixotic in Hunt's strange social freaks and fancies. He had the simplicity, the directness, the self-forgetfulness of a child. He would go up to a severe, austere Boston dignitary, who looked as if he had never been touched in his life, throw his arms around his neck and cry how glad he was to see him. He would mimic anything. If he had to tell a story of an elephant and a monkey, he would act the creatures till you saw and heard them. When he found a group of ladies knitting stockings, he begged a pair, put them on his hands with slippers, tied a white skirt round his neck, placed a table in front of him and a dark screen behind him, then with the slippered hands performed the evolutions of a graceful and accomplished dancer. And all these antics flowed out so gayly and naturally that no one could resist them.

At the same time, even more than in his aspect

or in his gayety, Hunt's social charm lay in his tongue. And keen and quick and pointed as the tongue was, it was not bitter. He hated sham and attacked it wherever he found it. He hated pretense and convention and indolent assumption of superiority. Of the idle rich he said: 'The people who live by accumulated wealth, with which they do nothing, are a set of lugs. The community carries them. Every time they die there's a song of angels.' And he had always such severity at command to wither the vain and the proud. But he had no small gossip, no petty epigram at the expense of others' feelings, did not depend for his wit upon the trivial catches of cruel smartness which make the clever social reputation of so many.

Likewise he was willing to listen as well as to talk, and this is a rare merit in those who talk well. When he was tired and depressed, and a friend told him some lively stories, he was delighted and exclaimed: 'I never heard so many wicked stories before in my life, and I should think you would not like to be alone with your Maker. The air is full of wickedness.' And he breathed it with huge relish.

But the charm was not in the listening, as it sometimes is. It was in the ever-varied, diversified, exhaustless, outpouring of wit and comment and suggestion and reflection on all sorts of persons and all sorts of subjects. The moods were there, as in every genuine and instinctive spirit. Sometimes Hunt would sit silent, looking far off, and perfectly indifferent to his surroundings. Sometimes he would realize his ineptitude and refuse to go into company at all. But in general he was ready and willing, and the slightest spark of matter would set him off into a quick, vivid, dazzling flow of sunny merriment or eloquence, which would make any company forget itself till the small hours of the morning. In the happy phrase of one who knew him well, 'It was an everyday expression of those who came in close contact with him that he "lighted up everything that he touched."'

III

It is by this gift of speech that we return to Hunt's passion for art, to his passion for beauty and for bringing beauty into the hearts and lives of others. During his later years in Boston, he was a notable figure, imparting to hundreds the enthusiasm that was all of life to him. He was a singularly inspiring teacher, and he gathered about him a cluster of pupils, to whom he communicated a zest for their work that clung to their whole lives, even if they had little or no genius. No doubt the pupils repaid him in an atmosphere of admiration and flattery, which was not always healthy. But Hunt was on the whole too manly and vigorous to be seriously spoiled by this.

His influence on his followers was positive and undeniable. He was not, indeed, a rigid and stern disciplinarian in emphasis upon the humbler elements of drawing. He had never been held to a severe apprenticeship in these himself, and some think that his work suffered from it. But for stimulus, for encouragement, for the instinctive analysis of a pupil's gifts and tendencies, there were few to equal him. He was quick to apply his darting wit to mockery of the business of teaching, as of everything else. 'Don't ask *me!* *I* don't know how. If I could find out how, I would go ten million miles on my knees to do it. We all want to know *how* things are done. Boston is a great place for receipts. There is a receipt for being scientific, one for being sentimental, another for being religious. But painting is something for which you can't get a receipt.' When he was annoyed, or bored, or perplexed, he could snub, and snub severely. A pupil said one day: 'When I copy anything at home, it looks very well; but when I get to the studio, whatever I do is not so good.' And Hunt's cool comment was: 'What do you suppose is the reason? Can it be that your work is not quite so good as you think it is?'

But in all the snubbing and all the mockery, the one main object was help, and Hunt never said a harsh word that he did not mean and feel to be constructive and clarifying. He believed that a large part of every artist's function was to teach others, and he was glad to give his time, his thought, his strength, to saving younger workers something of the unnecessary effort that he had been obliged to impose upon himself. 'I've been painting thirty years. Under instruction, I could, in ten years,

have learned all that I have learned — no, not all.
But I could have followed anyone in whom I had
confidence.' His two series of *Talks on Art* are as
brilliant, as illuminating, comment on the painter's
business as will be found anywhere. There is no
formulated theory. There is often contradiction
and inconsistency. But for intense, concentrated,
epigrammatic common sense the *Talks* are hard to
beat, as appears from the frequency with which I
have quoted them.

Labor? Does he want to teach his pupils labor?
He never taught them anything else, by precept or
by example. But he can indicate at once the in-
finity of labor and its limits, in a dozen words:
'All anybody can do is to *try*. Nobody ever does
anything. They only try.' Finish? He can teach
it, and he can mock at it: 'Most so-called "highly
finished" work is *hidebound*, and has that look of
goneness, that unmistakably empty look which a
house presents when the family have moved into
the country. Rotten-stone on the doorknob fails
to deceive.' And back of and through and over all
labor and finish he always emphasized the passion
of perception, the richness and fullness of spiritual
content, without which labor is trouble and finish
is vanity. 'Do *fascinating* things, not smart ones.
Nobody ever tucks a *smart* sketch under his arm
and runs home with it.' 'A quarter of an inch is
enough to disengage eternity on.' That infinite,
subtle, delicate, inexpressible, incomparable something, which makes all the difference, was always

hovering in his heart and in his brain, and his finest effort of speech was to make his pupils feel it: 'Spread the *light* on broadly as sunshine. But handle the passage from light into shadow as delicately as you would strew flowers upon a child's grave.'

Such an influence, such an enthusiasm, such a gift of words, must have worked far beyond the studio and the immediate students, must have had its leavening effect upon many who never came into direct contact with it. It is said that Hunt did not produce much impression upon contemporary artists, did not inspire a group, or found a school, as so many of the French painters did. He was too much of an individualist for this, too erratic and whimsical. But the passion of his worship of art must have spread far outside the limits of his narrow circle, must have somewhat profited a country which needed it then even more than it does today. He remarked once that 'painters shouldn't talk. They should have their mouths sewed up tight, and *do* the thing, not talk about it.' Well, he certainly gave his life to doing. But perhaps his talk availed his countrymen even more.

If he had not much sympathy with painters' critical talk, he had even less with the chatter of the professed critic. Artists generally are not too patient with those who cannot themselves create, but are always liberal with advice and comment for the laboring creator, and Hunt, who was patient in nothing except work, was no exception to the rule. I have no doubt he rejoiced in Sterne's humorous complaint, 'Of all the cants which are canted in this canting world, though the cant of hypocrites may be the worst, the cant of criticism is the most tormenting.' What Hunt resented was that critics would persist in taking a work of art for what it was not, instead of what it was. They set up a theoretical standard, to which nothing real ever attains or ever can, and then condemn a man's best for falling short of it. 'That is why criticism is so cruel,' he cries. 'It will not take any work of art for what it is worth. It is "a little too much this, and a little too much that," when the truth is, *nothing is right.*' And back of this was the still more fundamental defect, that the critic was thinking of himself, of his own cleverness, his own achievement, and not of the art or the artist that was before him. 'If art depended upon literature, there would never be much. The artist needs *help.* The critic should come to him in love, and seek to help him.'

The spirit of helpfulness is, I think, mainly apparent in Hunt's own comment on the work of others. There were certain artists and certain schools that did not appeal to him; but he did not discuss them, and when they were forced upon his notice, he evaded the subject and passed it by. He believed in being constructive, suggestive, stimulating always, or in keeping still. When it came to the great masters who had helped him, had taught him, his enthusiasm, while discriminating and

judicious, is as illuminating as it is immense. Of
Rubens, of Veronese, of Michelangelo he cannot
say enough. And as to Velasquez, the final object
of all painters' adoration, his simple word is
'Velasquez is beyond aspiring to.'

But the value of Hunt's influence shows, not so
much in his comment on individual artists or
pictures, as in his wide and infectious enthusiasm
for beauty, of whatever order and wherever found.
His countrymen in his day, perhaps in ours, were
engrossed with bread and butter, with blind,
material preoccupations, which made them indifferent to the exquisite resources of delight spread
so lavishly about them everywhere. Hunt shattered this indifference first of all by his own example. He had the fresh, perpetual, joyous ecstasy
of a child for all the little bits of loveliness to which
the weary, casual brain is utterly impervious.
Hear his charming words after recovery from an
illness: 'Everything is like flowers. Nobody knows
how happy I am in this coming from death to life,
with the perceptions of a tough old life joined to
the delicate sensitiveness of an infant. I don't
believe that anybody was ever so happy.... I see
flowers everywhere. Even a bit of blue rag in that
work-basket looks like a beautiful flower.' And he
preached constantly that beauty is in common
things, not in the remote or extraordinary, not in
far mountains or strange glaciers, or California, or
Patagonia, but right in your own dooryard and in
your own thoughts. 'The effect of light is what

makes things beautiful. Light never stops to find beauty. Half of the beautiful pictures in the world are painted from people who are not beautiful.'

Above all, Hunt's theory of art, and still more his instinctive feeling of it, was democratic. Beauty was not an exclusive possession, was not set apart for those of finer natures and subtler sensibilities. When he was doing his last great work in the Capitol at Albany, he was delighted with the workmen who crowded up to the scaffolding to see his pictures and told him that, while they were proud to be working on such a building, they were prouder still to see his work going on. 'I tell you,' said Hunt, 'that I never felt so big in my life as I did when they asked me if they could come again.' In his view beauty was not a question of large learning or many books, but of simply opening the eyes to see; and it was his function to open as many American eyes and touch as many American hearts as he could. Nobly did he labor to fulfill it. Whether he painted great things is beyond my competence to say; but that he loved great things, thought great things, and lived great things is quite indisputable.

VI

AN AMERICAN PEPYS
JOHN BEAUCHAMP JONES

CHRONOLOGY

JOHN BEAUCHAMP JONES
Born, Baltimore, Maryland, 1810.
First book, *Book of Visions*, published, 1847.
Established *The Southern Monitor*, Philadelphia, 1857.
A Rebel War Clerk's Diary at the Confederate States Capital,
published, 1866.
Died, 1866.

VI

AN AMERICAN PEPYS

I

SAMUEL PEPYS was an official of the British Navy. During the years from 1660 to 1670, he kept an extensive diary recording both private and public incidents and experiences. The element of general human revelation in this diary is perhaps most important; but it has also immense value to history, giving an inside comment upon the leading men, the course of public affairs, and the condition of English life and society at that time.

John Beauchamp Jones was a clerk in the War Department at Richmond during all the four years of the brief, intense, tragic struggle of the Southern Confederacy. And Jones kept a diary, not quite so elaborate as that of Pepys, but still minute and extensive enough to be of profound interest. In many respects he was well fitted for this task. Born in 1810, in the South, he was fifty years old when the Confederacy began its existence. He had traveled in Europe and in other parts of the world and seen all sorts of men and all sorts of conditions of life. He was a journalist by profession and a considerable author and he had the journalist's eager curiosity as to people and events. He was a married man with a family, settled to regular ways of life and not too much distracted by his own affairs from the impersonal consideration of what went on about him.

It must be said at once that he gives the impression of being distinctly a smaller man than Pepys. It is true that Pepys had his petty sides; but there is about him a simple directness, a spontaneous energy, an originality and spiritual freshness which amount to genius and remove him from the commonplace, for all he sometimes seems to wallow in it. John Beauchamp Jones was a much more conventional person and looked at life constantly from the angle of the staid, respectable Philistine, doing nothing, writing nothing, and thinking nothing that the Philistine conscience would not approve. No one need expect to find in him those moral irregularities which it is to be feared make a good deal of the attraction of Pepys for the casual reader. If Jones was conscious of peccadilloes, he did not go out of his way to set them down.

Nor had he Pepys's gift of expression. Pepys writes as carelessly and inadvertently as he or any man thinks; but he was a born stylist. Jones was much more correct, and he had had long practice with the pen. Yet the instinctive imaginative artist is not there. Now and then there is a touch that tells, as of Seddon, 'even in the moment of aspen consternation, he was still the politician'; or of Benjamin, 'upon his lip there seems to bask an eternal smile; but if it be studied, it is not a smile — yet it bears no unpleasing aspect.' But the usual level is that of somewhat commonplace journalism, and there are occasional outbreaks of rhetoric that are much worse than commonplace. 'The wrath of the Southern chivalry will some day burst forth on the ensanguined plain, and then let the presumptuous foemen of the North beware of the fiery ordeal they have invoked.' It is hard to imagine Pepys writing like that. At the same time, Jones, even as a writer, has his merits. He is at least generally brief, and his ordinary run of expression is far more simple, direct, terse, tense, and therefore Pepysian than that of Gideon Welles, whose opportunities for diary-writing in Washington were even greater.

But Jones's opportunities were great enough. In fact, when you take into account the immense importance of the events that were taking place about him, the picturesque and startling variety of life in Richmond during those bitter years, you feel that the material the man dealt with had even greater possibilities than that within the grasp of Pepys. And it is interesting to note that Jones fully appreciated this, and that from the beginning it was his object to make a day-to-day record which should have historical value for posterity. His definiteness of statement in this regard is far beyond anything in Pepys. Before he had even obtained any assured position, he writes: 'At fifty-one I can hardly follow the pursuit of arms; but I will write and preserve a diary of the revolution.' He explains clearly to the Secretary of War that his desire is 'employment and facilities to

preserve interesting facts for future publication.'
And the place he seeks is rather one that will be
helpful to this end than anything that will give
him distinction at the expense of leisure: 'I shall
be content to obtain the necessary position to
make a full and authentic diary of the transactions of the government.'

II

The first thing we look for in any diary is the
character of the diarist himself, for the purpose of
weighing his veracity, if for no other reason. It
cannot be said that Jones reveals his inmost soul
with quite the abundance or the candor of Pepys:
he had neither the inclination nor the faculty to do
so. Still, in the course of his eight hundred pages
he tells a great deal, both intentionally and unintentionally, and the man thus shown to us, if not
in all points attractive, is interesting and in the
main worthy of respect. As to those long fifty
years of earlier life he tells us little, being, as Pepys
was, too much occupied with immediate concerns.
Still, there are enough occasional references to show
that his main ambition had been that of authorship,
and a perusal of his numerous books proves that
that ambition was both active and to some extent
justifiable. He wrote novels which had apparently
a certain vogue in their day and which, when
glanced over now, diffuse the dusty, smothering
odor of oblivion that always emanates from ro-
mances of the past when not the product of endur-

ing genius. In these stories play-people in fantastic garments chatter endlessly and laugh with a ghastly dreariness, and one's spirit is clouded with vague depression to think that to this even the best-seller of 1925 must also come. The man had ingenuity of invention and he aped Dickens with a gross vivacity of humor, which should be remembered when one notes the utter lack of humor in the *Diary*. Also, one of his stories, *Wild Southern Scenes*, published in 1859, is curiously anticipatory of the war and all the disasters of secession and revolution.

At the age of fifty, the ambition had evidently grown somewhat pale, though it still lingers in the desire for the permanence of the *Diary*. If it took any political form, this was neither very sustained nor very active. And he deplores with a sigh his lack of knowledge of the arts which bring political success: 'Hereafter I shall study Gil Blas for the express purpose of being his antithesis. But I shall never rise until the day of doom brings us all to our feet again.'

During the *Diary* period, at any rate, Jones's life was in the daily routine of his office, and it is clear that he performed his duties faithfully and even zealously. Being no longer young, and by no means strong, he did not generally go out of his way to find extra work. When he is offered a somewhat higher place, he declines: 'I said I preferred a less conspicuous position — and less labor — but thanked him.' Yet he works persistently, system-

atically, and with intelligence. In the chaos of
an improvised public office, with inexperienced
political clerks intruding everywhere, the methodi-
cal efforts of a trained, thoughtful man must have
been welcome. Even when Jones asks and obtains
a vacation, he is usefully busy: 'Today I asked of
the department a month's respite from labor, and
obtained it. But I remained in the city, and
watched closely, still hoping I might serve the
cause, or at least prevent more injury to it.' When
other departments encroach upon his and attempt
to hamper him in the exercise of his functions, he
stands up to them with determined energy. The
provost-marshal threatens him with vengeance,
'if I granted any more passports to Petersburg
where he was military commander... I simply
uttered a defiance, and he departed, boiling over
with rage.' When the city is menaced by the
enemy and the official world is getting ready to fly,
he sticks to his post: 'I suppose the government
would go to Lynchburg. I shall remain with the
army *and see that the tobacco be burnt, at all hazards,
according to law.'*

The man seems to have been as devoted in
domestic duties as he was in public. His wife and
sons and daughters appear frequently in the
Diary, and the relations between them all were
amicable and helpful. No doubt there was more or
less of the friction unavoidable in any household,
but little trace of it appears in the record. On the
contrary, there is tenderness and consideration for

those present, and the absent are the object of constant longing and regret. For a time, especially at the beginning, difficulties of living in Richmond made it necessary for husband and wife to be separated. But during the later years, when help and comfort were most needed, they were together. What the charm of this family life was, I think appears most simply and touchingly in the references to various animal pets. When food was scarce and dear, the keeping of such creatures was a serious matter. Custis's parrot 'has accompanied the family in all their flights, and, it seems, will *never* die.' Fannie's cat departs at last, and the father's mixture of feelings has an almost Pepysian quality: 'My daughter's large pet cat died last night under the cherry tree, and was buried this morning under a rosebush. I sympathize with Fannie in the grief natural on such an occasion; but really the death of the cat in such times as these is a great relief to me, as he was maintained at the cost of not less than $200 per annum. His death was probably occasioned by a surfeit of meat which his mistress obtained unexpectedly, seeing it fall in the street, and sending a servant for it.'

As the above indicates, the stress and pressure of increasing money troubles are perhaps the features that stand out most in the personal side of the *Diary*. Jones seems to have had few resources outside of his salary, or what he had were wiped out in the general upheaval of financial and all other normal conditions. His salary was never magnificent, and, though several times enlarged, it was utterly inadequate to meet the strain of general inflation and war prices. There is some reference to service in the household and this means probably one or two slaves. But the work of all kinds was largely done by the family. Places of abode were scarce and rents were exorbitant. Furniture was hard to find and not substantial when found. In the course of time the Joneses managed to scrape together enough to get along with; but the results were somewhat incongruous: 'Thank Heaven! the little furniture, etc., we now have is our own — costing less to buy it than the rent we paid for that belonging to others up to the beginning of the month.... I think we have articles belonging in their time to twenty families.' The clothing problem was as troublesome as that of furniture. The simplest articles were difficult to obtain and obtainable only at almost prohibitive prices. Garments were worn as long as they would hold together, and a little longer: 'As for clothes, we are as shabby as Italian lazzaronis — with no prospect whatever of replenished wardrobe, unless some European power will come and take us, as the French have done Mexico.' And the question of food was even more serious and perplexing than that of clothes. With salt selling at seventy cents a pound, it will not be supposed that much indulgence in luxuries was possible. Occasionally some special delicacy brightened a day; but for the most part the simplest and coarsest foods were all that could be depended upon, and it was hardly practicable to get enough of those. 'Meantime we are in a half-starving condition. I have lost twenty pounds, and my wife and children are emaciated to some extent.' Yet with all this privation the diarist notes that the health of his family and on the whole that of the city generally is excellent, which seems to show that some,diminution of food might be beneficial to a good many of us. And, as in all such crises, the habit is quickly formed of living in the present hour and taking care of it, leaving the future to take care of itself: 'Although we scarcely know what we shall have tomorrow, we are merry and patriotic today.' Yet it is interesting to see how, under such bitter and cruel stress, even fairly patriotic spirits tend to look at the purely personal side of things. Jones makes arrangements to have supplies sent from North Carolina, and when he hears of Federal activities, he prays: 'I do sincerely hope Grant's raiders will keep quiet until *I* can get something to eat.'

In spite of the pressure, which was obviously so great, and of the temptations, which must have been many, there is no touch in the *Diary* from which one might infer any sort of dishonest or irregular procedure in its author, not even those dubious transactions in which Pepys was sometimes involved in accordance with the morals of his age. Jones speaks with the utmost bitterness of the sins of speculators and extortioners, and I see no reason to suppose that he himself sinned in the slightest degree, though perhaps his own honesty might have been compatible with a little more lenience toward the merely suspected dishonesty of others. He seems to have been strictly and decidedly conscientious, not only in money matters, but in all questions of underhanded and doubtful procedure: 'I hate all stratagems for the purpose of stimulating one to commit a wrong.' And in general he struggled with his difficulties as an honorable and upright man should do.

One looks curiously to see whether in the record of all this long four years of anxiety and suffering there was any sign of relaxation or amusement. There were such things to be had in Richmond at all times; but there seems to have been precious little of them in the Jones family. The descriptions of attempts at Christmas gayety are pathetic in their bare simplicity: 'We have quite a merry Christmas in the family; and a compact that no unpleasant word shall be uttered, and no *scramble* for anything.' On the very last Christmas of the war an old trunk is disinterred, the lock broken open, and family relics of dress and ornament appear which serve to rejuvenate the wardrobes and are distributed with something of holiday merriment. When the father of the family seeks diversion, he works in his garden or fishes in the brook for minnows large enough to be eaten on a pinch. And it is a curious illustration of the vicissitudes of this man's life that perhaps the best of his books is given to the account of whaling in the South

Pacific. It was a striking transition, from the most ample of all forms of sport, the chasing of sperm-whales in the boundless sea, to fishing for minnows with a bent pin in a threshold brook in Richmond. As there is little indication of amusement in the history of the Jones family, so there is little record of social life. Well-to-do Richmond people managed to keep up a good deal of activity of this sort. We see from Mrs. Chesnut's *Diary* that there were dances and masquerades and general social gatherings. Heaven knows, says Mrs. Chesnut in effect, we might be dismal to despair, but it seems wiser to keep our hearts up in this way. Yet the middle class, if the Jones family duly represent them, did not do much in the social line. The father goes to a presidential reception and makes brief comment on it; but there seems to be little paying or receiving of visits, little effort to seek comfort or oblivion in this way.

A surer form of refuge than could be found with humanity was spiritual belief and hope. Like the greatest of the Southern leaders, Lee, Jackson, Davis, and no doubt like a vast majority of the Southern people, John Beauchamp Jones was a firm and unfaltering believer in orthodox Christianity, and a constant practitioner — at least in intention — of its precepts. He even thinks it necessary to apologize for writing his diary on Sunday. No amount of suffering or disaster seems to arouse the slightest question as to the divine dispensation of affairs. Indeed, Jones's clearer vision does not assume, as is so usual, that the cause he adopts must necessarily have the divine support, though he hopes and prays for it: 'It is a dark hour. But God disposes. If we deserve it, we shall triumph; if not, why should we?' The action of Providence in special cases is accepted and asserted with a dogmatic definiteness somewhat startling to those who are accustomed to a vaguer view. Just when the financial prospect is darkest and the pressure almost unbearable, an offer of assistance turns up from an entirely unlooked-for quarter. How is it possible not to see the hand of Almighty God in such a happy coincidence? 'I accepted the sum on his conditions. This is the work of a beneficent Providence, thus manifested on three different occasions — and to doubt it would be to deserve damnation.'

Yet it is quite evident that the absence of melancholy, of a disposition to question the kindly government of the universe in moments of despair, is not owing to lack of sensibility. The man's nerves, on the whole, were finely strung, quick in their response to suffering and conditions of gloom, quick also in their sensitiveness to any form of beauty or charm. This appears most attractively in his appreciation of the loveliness of the natural world. He loves trees, and resents it when the enemy cut them down: 'What harm have the poor trees done...? I love trees, anywhere.' He makes himself a bit of a garden in his yard, cultivates every available spot, and spends long hours there.

The product of the garden is helpful and refreshing, but even more refreshing is the quiet solace of Nature's simplicity and innocence: 'My beets, tomatoes, early potatoes, and lettuce look pretty well, though not so far advanced, in consequence of the late spring, as I have seen them in Burlington. But they are a great comfort to me. I work them, water them, and look at them, and this is what the French would call a *distraction*. I have abundance of roses, this is the city of roses. And my cherries are coming on finely — I know not yet what kind they are; but it relieves the eye to gaze on them. And then my neighbor has a pigeon-house, and the birds come into my yard and are fed by my daughters, being pretty and tame. I sit for hours watching them.'

What is of greatest interest to us in the diarist is, of course, his intellectual grasp and ability, since upon these must depend the value of his interpretation of the great events that went on about him. It must be confessed at once that one does not get the impression of anything much above the average. Jones was well educated, he likes to read, does read, and especially has read, he handles a pen with facility, he has the journalist's quick and ready but superficial observation. Yet there is little profound or very original thinking on any subject. Perhaps a man of larger mental range would have been less adequate to render all the phases of what went on about him; but one cannot help feeling that the mental range is not always there. An interesting autobiographical meditation, written on the diarist's fifty-third birthday, may well close the portrayal of him as an individual: 'Hitherto I have dismissed from my mind, if not with actual indifference, yet with far more unconcern than at present, the recurring birthdays which plunged me farther in the vale of years. But now I cannot conceal from myself, if so disposed, that I am getting to be an old man. My hair is gray — but nevertheless my form is still erect, and my step is brisk enough. My fancies, tastes, and enjoyments have not changed perceptibly; and I can and often do write without glasses. I desire to live after this war is over, if it be the will of God — if not, I hope to exist in a better world.'

III

So, in the *Diary* of John Beauchamp Jones we have the reflection of one of the great crises in the history of the United States, and the history of democracy, and the history of the world, in a fairly bright and well-polished, but rather limited mirror. There is something so complete, so largely tragic, so finished and perfect in the rise, development, and downfall of the Southern Confederacy that it seems strange that no historian of great genius has yet made it the subject of a separate dramatic narrative. The material is there, the great events are there, the great figures are there, and there is just that embodiment of larger spiritual causes and movements, that strange, inextricable tangle of good and evil that are necessary to produce an historical tragedy of the most enthralling fascination and effectiveness. Certainly, if one regards this tragedy as a sort of Greek artistic conception, with its prologue in the confusion of prewar controversy and the provisional government at Montgomery, its climax at Gettysburg and Vicksburg, its long-drawn-out fourth act in the delays of 1864, and its fearful catastrophe in the fall of Richmond and the surrender of Lee, the constant, picturesque comment of Jones adequately fills the part of the chorus, and, though he is far from being highly poetical, the somewhat commonplace and average temper of his mind is not unlike that typified in the abstract choral figure of Greek tragedy.

The general application of our deductions as to his intellectual power, of course, finds its place all through the story. His philosophical reflections on what happens about him are not the most important part of his book. But he is often surprisingly acute and vivid in the observation and presentation of small matters. To take a more personal illustration: An officer comes one day on some personal matter. Jones talks with him, studies him, puts two and two together, finally notices that the officer curtsies when he leaves the room, and thereupon informs the authorities, who had all accepted him at his face value, that they are dealing with a woman. Again, he has a rather remarkable gift of making minor personages stand out. There is a pursy, puffy, officious, inefficient colonel who clings in the reader's memory almost like an office-mate of Pepys. And the same gift is applied even more impressively to figures of greater distinction and importance. Secretary Seddon, 'who usually wears a sallow and cadaverous look, which, coupled with his emaciation, makes him resemble an exhumed corpse after a month's interment, looks today like a galvanized corpse which had been buried two months. The circles round his eyes are absolutely black.' Or there will be a scene which thrills you almost as if you saw it, a scene of horror or a scene of heroism, like that of the boy of fifteen who holds out his hand with a bullet in the wrist, and says, smiling, 'I'm going to the hospital just to have the ball cut out, and will then return to the battle-field. I can fight with my right hand.'

As regards the general merits of the Confederate cause, it is hardly necessary to say that Jones is thoroughly orthodox. Though he has lived much in the North, his loyalty to Southern principles is not in the least affected. 'This is a holy cause we are embarked in,' he cries, 'worthy to die for.' The sacred theory of State Rights, as preached by Calhoun and Davis, the integrity of the Constitution as established by the fathers, these must be maintained against the encroaching North with every sacrifice of blood and treasure and happiness. Slavery, too, is not only a useful institution, but a necessary institution, even a divinely ordained institution. It must be clung to at any cost. And as it is better for the whites, so it is past question better for the blacks. 'The negroes are the best-clad people in the South.... They are well-fed, too ... and present a happy appearance. And they are happy. It is a great mistake of the Abolitionists, in supposing the slaves hail their coming with delight; on the contrary, nearly all the negroes regard their approach with horror.'

At the same time, Jones, like many other political thinkers, saw from the very beginning the weakness of the Confederate position, which was emphasized by even the President's wife at a little later period. It was hopeless to try to carry on a long war, to build a vigorous military government on such a basis of shifting sand as the theory of State Rights. Centralization, concentration, became more and more necessary. As Jones expresses it in the early months, 'Many are inclined to think the safest plan will be to obliterate State lines, and merge them all into an indivisible nation or empire, else there may be incessant conflicts between the different sovereignties themselves, and between them and the General Government.' Even if it came to a sheer military control, where would be the harm? 'Like the Russian, perhaps, we shall have a purely military government; and it may be as good as any other.' Nay, a straight-out monarchy would be more acceptable than submission to the detested Yankees: 'If we are to have a monarchy for the sake of economy and stability, I shall submit to it in preference to the domination of the Northern radicals.'

As the war progressed and Jones became more assured in his position, as his steadiness and cool common sense began to make themselves felt, it is interesting to see him quietly putting forward practical suggestions, just as Pepys did, and getting them considered and sometimes even accepted by men of far greater prominence than he. In the early stages he ventures to predict somewhat freely as to the danger of giving passports to persons wishing to go North. He is told that such talk is rash and will bring him to ruin, if his prediction is not verified. 'I reply that I would rather be destroyed than that it should be fulfilled.' Later on, he takes it upon himself to suggest to the President directly that an appeal should be made to the people to furnish supplies of various kinds. But even in making the suggestion he realizes that it will be of no avail. Official routine is too overpowering: 'Red tape will win the day, even if our cause be lost. Our soldiers must be fed and clothed according to the "rules and regulations," or suffer and perish for the want of food and clothing.' Later still, he urges upon the Secretary of War the necessity of organizing non-conscripts for local defense, and to this suggestion he receives a positive response that it would be followed. But long experience makes him skeptical: 'Today I received the reply saying it would be done. But will the *arms* be distributed among them?' Yet, in spite of indifference and rebuffs, he persists to the end, in giving advice, often intelligent advice, and the more intelligent of his superiors are prepared to listen to him.

Situated as he is, he has, of course, immense advantages for judging these same superiors, for appraising not only their manifest actions, but their intimate quality and power. In the early days he is naturally full of enthusiasm. Some of the politicians, to be sure, are dubious; but he hopes that they will be quickly understood and got rid of. And what a group of distinguished men the great cause has to choose from. There are the two Johnstons. There is Beauregard, who has 'great genius and is perhaps the most dashing and brilliant officer in the country.' There is Toombs, who declaimed upon the splendid possibilities of the future and the plan that ought to be pursued: 'And as he warmed with the subject, the *man* seemed to vanish, and the *genius* alone was visible.' There is Jackson, a professor and an odd one; but 'I hope he will take the field himself; and if he does, I predict for him a successful career.' Best of all, there is Lee, who 'should have command of the largest army in the service, for his is one of the most capacious minds we have.' As to the President, whom Jones approached closely at an early stage, the progress of comment is most interesting. But the first impression is decidedly favorable, though a shrewd finger is laid upon the weak point: 'The features of his face are distinctly marked with character; and no one gazing at his profile would doubt for a moment that he beheld more than an ordinary man.... There is nothing sinister or repulsive in his manners or appearance; and if there are no special indications of great grasp of intellectual power on his forehead and on his sharply defined nose and chin, neither is there any evidence of weakness, or that he could be easily moved from any settled purpose.... As a politician he attaches the utmost importance to *consistency* — and here I differ with him. I think that to be consistent as a politician is to change with the circumstances of the case.' But, whatever the weak points, the diarist affirms with entire truth, 'So far, perhaps, no Executive had ever such cordial and unanimous support of the people as President Davis.'

For from the repeated choral touches of this sympathetic observer one gathers overwhelmingly the tragic sense of a whole people rushing with unlimited confidence and swelling enthusiasm toward their utter destruction. The war would be a mere triumphal progress, and those encroaching, tyrannous, despotic Yankees would be taught what it meant to trespass upon the liberty of a free people. To be sure, Jones himself had lived in the North and knew its temper, and predictions as to the brevity of the war did not impress him so much as some others. But he, like the rest, is absolutely convinced that such heroic loyalty and devotion as he sees about him can never be suppressed or subdued. The Yankees may try as long as they like, but in the end they will be utterly discomfited. With the early victories this exultant assurance reaches the point of military mania. The heroic fighting spirit of the South must necessarily carry all before it. Even with defeat, even as the difficulties and obstacles increase, the courage and the confidence are not broken: 'Our enemies ought to know that, under almost any conceivable adverse circumstances, we can maintain the war twenty years.' And no doubt this note grows somewhat weaker as time goes on. The confidence has to be spurred and lashed a little to be maintained at its proper level. Yet the old fire is there, and the least breeze of successful conflict is sufficient to stir it into flame. In August, 1864, when the last real hope centred upon the defeat of Lincoln at the polls, Jones writes: 'Thank God, the prospect of peace is "bright and brightening," and a dark cloud is above the horizon in the North. Lincoln and his party are now environed with dangers rushing upon them from every direction.' And in February, 1865, little more than a month before Lee's surrender, there is still the suggestion of belief that escape is at least possible: 'We have some millions in gold... to purchase subsistence; and it is believed Virginia alone, for *specie*, can feed the army. Then *another* army may arise in Grant's rear.' So persistent and indomitable is the function of hope in those who should know that their fate is before them.

IV

Yet the element of gathering and constantly increasing tragedy is undoubtedly what obtains most and prevails in this striking and significant record. Even in the very early days we get foreshadowings and anticipations of it. When his ardent friends proclaim their certainty of triumph, Jones shakes his head. Years of experience have convinced him that all Northerners are not cowards and fools: eager partisans have 'no idea that the Yankees would *dare* to enter upon such enterprises in the face of an enlightened world. But I know them better. And it will be found that they will learn how to fight, and will not be afraid to fight.' In all the clamor of joy and exultation of temporary success, little murmurs of distrust and uncertainty may be heard. 'If we are not utterly crushed before May (an impracticable thing), we shall win our independence.' Independence must be maintained, it must at all costs; but still peace is so lovely and desirable: 'Oh, that peace would return! But with *Independence!*' And as time goes on, the expression of doubt becomes franker and more direct: 'I hope for the best, even if the worst is to come.'

It is most impressive to watch the tide of distress and misery creeping gradually upward and upward through these graphic pages, to witness the inevitable oncoming of disaster and despair. Perhaps nothing makes this advance more scientifically evident than the valuable statistical tables which Jones sets down at irregular intervals, displaying the steady increase in the price of all the necessaries of life. Luxuries rise and rise until they sail out of the sight of all but the very rich. The simple, indispensable articles grow daily scarcer and dearer. Clothes get hardly obtainable. Flour comes to fifteen hundred dollars a barrel, and most people have to substitute corn meal, finding it difficult to get even that. The cause of the trouble is partly the actual scarcity of food and the difficulty of distributing it; partly the extortion of the various speculators, which the diarist brands early and often, partly the constantly increasing disarrangement of the finances and immense depreciation of the currency. But whatever the cause, the poor have to suffer. 'We see men and women and children in the streets in dingy and dilapidated clothes; and some seem gaunt and pale with hunger — the speculators and thieving quartermasters and commissaries only looking sleek and comfortable.' Or, if you want a concrete and vivid picture of the way the thing works, take the story of the poor woman who went to a merchant to purchase flour. When he demanded an exorbitant price, she cried in agony, 'My God! how can I pay such prices? I have seven children; what shall I do?' And the merchant answered her, coolly, 'I don't know, madam, unless you eat your children.'

Sometimes the people tried to forget, sought oblivion in abnormal excitement. The theatres were always open and gambling reached scandalous or, if you like, pitiful proportions. Sometimes the murmurs approached the climax of actual rebellion and at the critical moment the mob broke loose and tried to help themselves to the stores which the speculators had accumulated. Jones describes the beginning of the riot with terrible, simple earnestness: 'Not knowing the meaning of such a procession, I asked a pale boy where they were going. A young woman, seemingly emaciated, but yet with a smile, answered that they were going to find something to eat. I could not, for the life of me, refrain from expressing the hope that they might be successful; and I remarked they were going in the right direction to find plenty in the hands of the extortioners.' It required the presence of the President himself, with all his most persuasive eloquence, to allay the disorder. But for the most part men and women endured with grim patience, hoped when they could, bore as they must, and sustained the cause, if not the government, with an admirable and astonishing fortitude. Jones repeatedly notes that, in spite of the suffering, there were no beggars anywhere.

But it engendered a terrible bitterness, a bitterness which even yet has not wholly faded away. There was the bitterness toward the enemy. The hideous Yankees are cruel, traitorous, murderous. The world would be well rid of them, if only it might be rid of them. Jones quotes the bitterness of others and adds plenty of his own: 'The universal education, so much boasted of in New England, like their religion, is merely a humbug, or worse than a humbug, the fruitful source of crime.... Ignorance is bliss in comparison with Yankee wisdom.' 'We have *awful* good news from New York: an *insurrection*, the loss of many lives, extensive pillage and burning, with a suspension of the conscription.'

Even worse, at any rate more tragic and pitiable, is the bitterness toward friends, the tendency, so human in misfortune, to blame everybody, even those who are doing their best to accomplish the impossible. There is mistrust everywhere, suspicion everywhere, accusations of all sorts flying blindly. It is so vastly easier to criticize, to scold, to quarrel, than to work for the common good and keep silent. And Jones reflects the universal complaints, and adds to them, and typifies them. There is complaint of measures, of the handling of passports, of the handling of conscriptions, of the handling of supplies, and of trade and finance. There is the cry of favoritism, so sure to arise, so likely to be well founded, so difficult to prove. There is the complaint of general incapacity, again terribly natural, since the huge task of government is beyond human power in normal times and in abnormal becomes too great for even giants to wrestle with.

Everywhere in the *Diary* there surges up the crowd of active figures, who are made the subject of analysis, criticism, and fault-finding. First it is the minor personages, whose doings come more closely within the diarist's observation and whose misdoings he can blame more freely. The military field is, of course, not so much within his reach, but even here his comments are frequent and suggestive. He reflects the popular prejudice for success: 'I have almost a superstitious faith in *lucky* generals, and a corresponding prejudice against unlucky ones, and their progeny.' When the military men begin to operate close at hand, he has quarrel enough with them. The provost-marshal, General Winder, is an ogre simply, a monster of malice and meanness and stupidity. The commissary general, Northrop, a favorite of the President, is a creature of red tape and routine. He predicts disaster if his pet plans are not exactly followed. Disaster comes, 'and when I saw him afterward, his face was lit up with triumph, as if he had gained a victory. He *predicted* it, because they would not let him impress all the food in the country.'

When it comes to the office-holders, the lesser political personages whom Jones saw about him every day, he does not stint his outcry against their dishonesty and inefficiency. No doubt there are exceptions, but those, alas, are not the ones who get talked of. Congress? Nobody has ever yet, that I know of, commended the Confederate Congress as a capable body, and Jones graphically displays the defect: 'In future times I wonder if it will be said that we had great men in this Congress? Whatever may be *said*, the truth is, there are not a

dozen with any pretensions to statesmanship.'
Red tape? The world seems bound up with it.
Little rules, narrow regulations, stupid system,
mingled with still stupider lack of system, entangle
and confuse everybody and everything. Worst of
all is the sense of dishonesty. The speculators and
profiteers are everywhere. 'Even adroit clerks are
becoming wealthy. They procure exemptions, dis-
charges, and contracts for the speculators for heavy
bribes,... indifferent to the fate of the country, so
that their own prosperity be secure. After the war
the rascals and traitors will be rich, and ought to be
marked and exposed.'

Then gradually the criticism creeps upward from
the small fry to the greater men who ought to be
immune from it. And again with the military leaders the fault-finding is less marked. Indeed, Jones
often proclaims his confidence as to the army in the
field, both high and low. The people will fight and
work, and they would save the country if the politicians would let them. Yet, even with the generals,
criticism is not altogether silent. Men like Cooper
and G. W. Smith may be freely accused of derelic-
tion in duty. When things look very dark, Lee himself, though persistently admired and commended,
does get a shadow of blame, at least in the minds of
the undiscerning: 'Even Lee's great name is dimmed
somewhat in the estimation of fools. He must beat
Meade before Grant comes up, or suffer in reputation.'

When it is a question of the leading politicians

and would-be statesmen, the blame is unsparing and often savage. Randolph and Seddon are well-meaning but inefficient and always subservient to the President. Benjamin, Memminger, Mallory are not perhaps actually dishonest. But they are woefully beneath the dignity and greatness of the cause they undertake to serve, and above all they look out for their own ease and comfort and enjoyment before they think of the needs of the country and the dangers of the future. The following passage as to a dinner given by the Secretary of the Navy is but typical: 'Mr. Mallory's red face, and his plethoric body, indicate the highest living; and his party will enjoy the dinner while so many of our brave men are languishing with wounds, or pining in a cruel captivity. Nay, they may feast, possibly, while the very pillars of the government are crumbling under the blows of the enemy.' And another terribly severe general indictment represents the feeling of many besides the diarist, as they grew more and more discouraged and desperate: 'Never before did such little men rule such a great people. Our rulers are like children or drunken men riding docile horses, that absolutely keep the riders from falling off by swaying to the right and left, and preserving an equilibrium. There is no rule for anything and no stability in any policy.'

And what about the man who was the chief of all, the protagonist, you might almost say the Prometheus of this enormous drama, Jefferson Davis? We have seen that in the beginning Jones admired his chief, appreciated his powers, and really hoped that he would be equal to the great part he had to play. But as time went on, the enthusiasm waned. There was always personal respect, always the conviction that Davis was thoroughly honest and patriotic and a man of force and genius in certain sides of his character. But — well, he was simply unequal to a task which would perhaps have been too much for any man; and Jones sums the matter up in effective fashion: 'The President is considered really a man of ability, and eminently qualified to preside over the Confederate States, if independence were attained and we had peace. But he is probably not equal to the rôle he is now called upon to play. He has not the broad intellect requisite for the gigantic measures needed in such a crisis, nor the health and physique for the labors devolving upon him. Besides, he is too much of a politician to discard his old prejudices, and persists in keeping aloof from him and from commanding positions all the great statesmen and patriots who contributed most in the work of preparing the minds of the people for resistance to Northern domination.... The disaffection is intense and widespread among the politicians of 1860, and consternation and despair are expanding among the people.'

They continued to expand, until disaffection from within and disaster from without became so overwhelming that they dragged down Prometheus headlong, and with him the tremendous fabric which he and millions of others had striven so desperately to rear. The disaster was ruinous, all-involving, complete, and as a mere minor incident it wipes out forever the diarist John Beauchamp Jones, first as a diarist and shortly after as a man. On the fifth of April, 1865, four days before the surrender of Lee, Jones writes: 'Three P.M. I feel that this diary is near its end.' On the tenth, the day after the surrender, he writes: 'My diary is surely drawing to a close, and I feel as one about to take leave of some old familiar associate.' And the last entry, perfectly simple and unpretentious, seems to me to conclude the choral office with tragic significance and effectiveness: 'April nineteenth — Yesterday windy, today bright and calm. It appears that the day of the death of President Lincoln was appointed for illuminations and rejoicings on the surrender of Lee. There is no intelligence of the death of Mr. Seward or his son. It was a dastardly deed — surely the act of a madman.'

VII.
JONES VERY

CHRONOLOGY

JONES VERY
Born in Salem, Massachusetts, August 28, 1813.
Graduated at Harvard College, 1836.
Teacher of Greek at Harvard, 1836–1838.
Essays and Poems, published, 1839.
Died at Salem, May 8, 1880.

JONES VERY

VII

JONES VERY

'THE sentiment which inspires your poetry is so deep and true, and the expression so simple, that I am sure you will find your audience very large.' So wrote Emerson to Jones Very in the year 1838. With *Parnassus* in one's hand, one may hardly feel inclined to pay great respect to Emerson's critical dicta. Neither has public opinion on this case done much to sustain him. Where one hears a thousand times the names of Longfellow and Whittier, one hardly hears the name of Very once; and I suppose one copy of his poems does not sell to a hundred of theirs. Yet, in spite of this, I cannot but think Emerson's opinion worth consideration. Certain qualities of Very's writings, if one examines them, go far to justify it.

For biographical details I must frankly acknowledge myself indebted to the notice which Mr. Andrews, a most painstaking and appreciative editor, prefixed to his edition of Jones Very's poems. As there are some men whose lives are their greatest work, so there are others whose work constitutes their lives. Very seems to me one of this latter class; and how or where he lived becomes, therefore, a matter of but slight importance, a mere framework to the building which grew out of his spirit.

JONES VERY

The history of his boyhood and youth seems not to have been characterized by anything of special note. An intense love of study, fostered, perhaps, rather than opposed by circumstances which tended to throw him upon another sphere of life, led to his pushing his way through many difficulties to college. There, Mr. Andrews tells us, he not only distinguished himself much as a scholar, but impressed all who came into contact with him by the gentleness and purity of his life. There, also, and still more in the Divinity School, which he entered after leaving college, he began to show that peculiarly religious side of his character which afterwards manifested itself in all that he did. I should be glad to quote freely from Mr. Andrews here, and even to quote much that he has quoted, touching the delicate and subtle manifestations of the Spirit in this man; but for all that I must send the reader to the book itself. My purpose is only to allude in passing to the singular and almost prophetic isolation in which Very lived, and the sort of affectionate and reverent awe he inspired even in those who knew him best.

Three editions of Very's writings have been published — the first by the agency of Emerson, in 1839; the second, consisting only of the poems, which I have already alluded to, by Mr. Andrews, in 1883; and the third, *Poems and Essays*, in 1886. The first contains three prose essays and about fifty poems and sonnets, the second is a republication of the poems with the addition of about fifty sonnets collected from various sources, and the interesting notice mentioned above. I shall speak first of the prose; because, while it is filled with the same spirit which pervades the poetry, and so forms a good introduction to that, I myself do not find in it the same artistic touch, the same lightness and ease which make the charm of the verse. The difference is that between a man's working with tools for which he was born, and again with others which are not natural to him.

When, however, we come to examine the three essays, in the order in which they are printed, we shall find between the first and last of them something of the same difference which exists between the prose as a whole and the verse; so much so, indeed, that one might almost conceive of a gradual progress from one to the other, and believe that the genius of the man had in this way followed its own law of development. It is true that a comparison of dates will hardly bear us out in this view; and yet, so often, the internal life cannot be measured by the times and limits of the external: one may see the youth and the man dwelling in the same soul side by side. And it seems to me that the history of many minds can be understood and written only by a chronology of the spirit different from that of the body.

The essay on Epic Poetry, in this order, comes to us first; and here, I believe, we have the earliest of Very's works, both in its manner and in its date. In this he attempts to prove that the epic, from its

nature, belongs to a past age and all efforts to re-
produce it under modern conditions must fail. He
has put originality into his work. Even here, we
begin to find a theory of poetry, a theory of life,
entirely new. Already Very has begun to treat nature and the human soul in his own way, viewing
everything in the relation which his own mind had
established between itself and God:

'The effect of Christianity was to make the individual mind the great object of regard, the centre of
eternal interest, and transferring the scene of action
from the outward world to the world within, to give
all modern literature the dramatic tendency — and
as the mind of Homer led him to sing of the physical conflicts of his heroes with *visible* gods *without*;
so the soul of the modern poet, feeling itself con-
tending with motives of Godlike power *within*,
must express that conflict in the dramatic form, the
poetry of sentiment.'

Here and elsewhere one touches the note which
makes Very true and noble: his insight into the history and nature of the soul. The inquiry in regard
to Epic Poetry, moreover, does not lack interest.
And yet one feels a certain sense of effort through it
all. It is the work of a man born to affirm and not
to compare; and affirmation is not the office of
criticism. The style, too, is weak. One finds occasionally a strong, nervous sentence after the manner of Emerson, a manner so easily caught by those
who read him, and so dangerous to anyone who cannot use it. Yet this manner, keen, trenchant, vigor-

ous, is not Very's own: it has not grace enough, has not enough of the true artist's touch. What Very's manner is, we shall see best when we come to his poetry, but in this first essay the style is tentative, doubtful, perhaps hampered by the same sense of effort which one cannot but feel in the matter of the piece also:

'The poets of the present day who would raise the epic-song, cry out like Archimedes: "Give me a place to stand on and I will move the world."'

To write like that is not to have a bad style. It is worse: to have no style at all. And Very's first essay is full of such sentences.*

When we come to his essays on Shakespeare and Hamlet, we are treading on other ground. If the same defects of manner are occasionally visible, one cannot help feeling that the man is speaking with an inspiration. And to an inspiration can we not pardon anything? The two essays may very well be considered together. They are both of them a development in the same line of the one idea that was beginning to take possession of Very's life: the idea that the human soul had no object and no aim but to identify itself with God, that in this union of our

* A curious coincidence occurs in this essay on Epic Poetry. Very writes, speaking of Milton: 'He could not adopt altogether the material or the immaterial system, and he therefore took his stand on the then debatable ground.' In Macaulay's essay on Milton we read: 'It was impossible for the poet to adopt altogether the material or the immaterial system. He therefore took his stand on the debatable ground.'
Did Very quote unconsciously? One would hardly think Macaulay much in his line.

will with his was to be found the satisfaction, the highest fulfillment of all desires. Without that, as he thinks, we must be forever miserable, all the more miserable, if we are ignorant of the cause of our pain.

I should be glad to quote all that Mr. Andrews says in regard to Very's view of Shakespeare. It seems that someone, mockingly disposed, offered the great dramatist as an example of genius, inspiration, without submission to the will of God. It set Very thinking. He made Shakespeare for a long time his especial study. To Emerson we are indebted for a few of his utterances on the subject, given in Emerson's own emphatic language.

'"Genius," said Very, "was the decay of Wisdom. To the preëxistent Shakespeare, Wisdom was offered; but he did not accept it and so he died away into Genius. When his Vineyard was given him, God looked that he should bring forth grapes, but he brought forth sour grapes." "But," said the interrogator, "My grapes tasted sweet." He replied: "That was because you knew not the sweet. All things are sweet until there comes a sweeter."'

The two essays of which we are speaking tend in the same line to prove that Shakespeare, like external nature, performed unconsciously the will of God; but even by that unconsciousness does he lose in greatness according to Very.

'By doing this,' he says — that is, showing Shakespeare to have lived unconsciously in the will of God — 'I shall show that there is a higher action than that we witness in him when the will has not been borne down and drawn along by the mind's own original impulse, but, though capable of resistance, yields flexibly to all its natural movements, presenting that higher phenomenon which genius and revelation were meant to forward in all men.'

That is the keynote. Everything is tuned to that. And again:

'We look upon such minds as Shakespeare's as exceptions, for wise purposes, to our common nature, and as the single man who is born blind tells thousands that there is One who giveth them sight, so those of our race, who by nature are so strongly prompted to will and to do that their minds seem almost as passive as matter beneath superior power, have been denied, to some extent, the liberty of will, as I think, that the many might be continually reminded that their minds were not their own, and that the conscious submission of their wills to the same great influence was their highest glory.'

At least the thesis is original. I do not think that the riddle of Avon has been tried in that way before. Certainly I do not say that Very has solved it; but in trying to explain Shakespeare, he explains himself. That is all we ask of him.

In the same strain he continues. Genius is but an increased activity, a more universal capacity for growth, a larger unconscious sympathy with all nature, animate and inanimate. It is by this that Shakespeare felt as he did the harmony between the evil and the good which must be unperceived by us:

'Like the ocean his mind could fill with murmuring waves the strangely indented coast of human existence from the widest bay to the smallest creek; then, ebbing, retire within itself, as if form was but a mode of its limitless and independent being.'

Shakespeare, too, in Very's idea of him, though hating decay and all the outward signs of death, though thrilled perpetually with the joy and beauty of the world, felt instinctively the eternity of his existence, felt it, perhaps, the more by reason of the passionate life that was within him. Hence his indifference to fame and his carelessness in the preservation of his works. 'For,' says Very, 'fame can only be a motive to those who have no practical belief in the next world, or to whom it is an uncertainty.' Certainly that is cutting the knot; but, after all, weaker explanations have passed current for the same thing.

But I am delaying too long. I must only allude in passing to the comparison which is instituted between Shakespeare and Milton:

'We look in vain, therefore, in Shakespeare, for that consciousness of the unconquerable will, which we find in Milton. Shakespeare could never have given us a character like Satan's."

And Very goes on to mark the difference which consists in Shakespeare's power of depicting life as it really is, as he sees it about him, while he is incapable of creating an ideal outside of life. The difference is clear, and the distinction not new. It is the explanation which is new and worth our attention, as it seems to me.

'Homer and Shakespeare were without a struggle the natural representatives of this action; and their language was a universal one through which all things found expression.... Such minds, as we have before said, seem to be exceptions, for wise purposes, to the rest of our race; exhibiting to all the natural features of the soul in the unconscious and childlike state of innocence.... In Wordsworth and Milton, on the contrary, we see the struggle of the child to become the perfect man in Christ Jesus. Their constant prayer is, "Not my will, Father, but thine be done." They are striving for that silence in their own bosoms, that shall make the voice that created all things heard.'

There are people who will call this fantastic. In truth, it is not the tone of America in the twentieth century, yet I cannot but think there is something near Christianity in it, nearer, perhaps, than some of us dream.

I must quote one passage more before we leave this essay, as much for the style, which shows Very's prose at its best, clear and refined, though never vigorous, as for the summing up of his idea of Shakespeare which it presents:

'Shakespeare, though at times he may have been possessed of his genius, must, in far the most numerous of his days and years, have been pos-

sessed by it. Lost in wonder at the countless beings that thronged uncalled the palace of his soul
and dwelt beneath its "majestical roof fretted with
golden fires"; he knew not, or, if he knew, forgot
that even those angel visitants were not sent for
him merely to admire and number; but that knowing no will but His who made kings His subjects,
he should send them forth on their high mission,
and with those high resolves which it was left for
him to communicate. Had he done this, we might,
indeed, reverence him as the image of his God; as
a sharer in His service, whose service is perfect
freedom.'

I do not say that that is great, but it is the work
of a man who had thought and felt. Many of us
may learn something from it.

I have quoted enough to show the vein. In the
essay on Hamlet, it is in the main points the same.
There is the same interest for us that there was in
the essay on Shakespeare: a new and strong interpretation of a hackneyed subject. And that is a
great recommendation here and today. There is
the same explanation of external phenomena by
internal, of the world by the soul. There is the
same depth and seriousness of treatment. Only,
perhaps, here the author is further advanced. He
has grown more at ease with his materials. He
begins to find himself at home.

To Very's mind, as to that of all critics, Hamlet
is the sun, the efflorescence of Shakespeare's genius;
but the application of Very's theory in regard to

this genius makes clear in Hamlet many things which have puzzled others. In Hamlet, he thinks, we have Shakespeare for a minute stopping to question this mighty stream of activity which elsewhere glows forth in him unbounded and unchecked. He stops suddenly. He examines himself. He asks himself the why of all these things; and the very power he has of feeling everything makes the question more tremendous, more unanswerable. According to Very, it is the great defect of Shakespeare that he cannot find the answer. All the disorder, all the ugliness, which is caused by the separation of the soul from God — this man could understand it all. But the solution of the riddle was not given to him.

Fantastic again! Fantastic or not, is there not thought here?

One thing only I must turn to here for a minute. It is the curious lack of taste which Very so often shows. In the end of this essay, for instance, quoting the noble speech of Prospero in *The Tempest*, he concludes it with the following:

> But hence retire me to my Avon where
> Every third thought shall be my grave.

Such things only show how utterly he lacked literary talent, which should be, as it were, the valet of genius, to keep its outward garment brushed and orderly.

I have spoken thus at length of Very's prose, because in it one sees the man apart from the artist, and it is interesting to begin with that. It is not often that one has a chance to see so clearly the foundation before one examines the structure that is built on it, and the opportunity should be improved when it comes. But the beauty and the charm are not there after all. One must go higher for them.

In our study of the poetry, we will turn at once to Mr. Andrews's edition. Everything is here which is to be found in the former edition, if I mistake not; and many things of the highest value which are not to be found there. I do not know who is responsible for the division and arrangement of the sonnets; but in that one point I prefer the former edition. Otherwise, I should be satisfied not to see it again.

Sainte-Beuve, speaking of Maurice de Guérin, observes delicately that the worship of Nature and the worship of Christ cannot go together: 'The Cross bars more or less the free view of Nature; the divine Pan has nothing to do with the divine crucified One.' At first sight, Very, like Wordsworth and some others, may seem a contradiction of this; but I do not think we shall find it so if we look carefully. True, he speaks again and again of Christ, often with love and almost adoration; and yet, to me he does not seem to look upon him as Christians looked upon him two hundred years ago. Jesus is to him a friend, a teacher, a brother, nay, in a certain sense, a savior, if you will; never, I think, a God. For God he looks above Calvary and beyond it, or rather he looks forward and not back, within and not without. In his idea, the God in Christ is in us too. 'He does not make Christ a man, but all men Gods,' or, better, part of God. Certainly, if this is not so, Sainte-Beuve is, in this case, wrong. First and foremost in Very comes his love of Nature, his power of interpreting her; and though, at minutes, he separates himself from her, feels an enmity between her and God, he always returns to her. She is his hope, his consolation, the real mediator between him and the divine:

> Nature! my love for thee is dearer far
> Than strength of words, though spirit-born, can tell.

That is the note. Again and again he turns to it. The best of his poems deal with it directly, and in all the others it is the ground-tone running through, side by side with his passionate desire to be at one with God. Indeed, his longing for Nature becomes often the best expression for this desire which he can find.

The first three divisions of the poems, which are made in the edition of 1883 — 'The Call,' 'The New-Birth,' 'The Message' — are concerned chiefly with the peculiar mission which he felt himself called to, and its communication to others. In 'The Call' he speaks repeatedly of his newly discovered communion with God, of the joy and peace which is to be found there:

> So does my spirit wait thy presence now
> To pour thy praise in quickening life along,

JONES VERY

Chiding with voice divine man's lengthened sleep,
While round the unuttered Word and Love their vigils keep.

Observe here the lengthening of the last line, an
innovation common in Very's sonnets, which adds
a certain largeness, as it seems to me. One sees in
this and in many other places in this part of the
book that peculiar sense of his own inspiration
which makes Very so remarkable. It is not the
confidence of Petrarch: 'Know me whoever can, I
know myself.' Nor is it the confidence of Shakespeare:

> For I am that I am, and they that level
> At my abuses reckon up their own.

Compared with that, one might almost call it the
confidence of Jesus:

> To him who hath, to him my verse shall give,
> And he the more from all he does shall gain.

And again:

> And men would own it was thy hand that blest,
> And from my bosom find a surer rest.

> And canst thou tell then where my journeying lies?
> If so, thou tread'st with me the same blue skies.

Confidence toward men, but the deepest humility
toward God, and all his confidence rooting itself
in this humility:

> O, humble me! I cannot bide the joy,
> That in my Saviour's presence ever flows,
> May I be lowly, lest it may destroy
> The peace his childlike spirit ever knows,

I would not speak thy word, but by Thee stand,
While Thou dost to thine erring children speak.
Oh, help me but to keep his own command,
And in my strength to feel me ever weak,
Then in thy presence shall I humbly stay,
Nor lose the life of love he came to give;
And find at last the life, the truth, the way
To where with Him thy blessed servants live;
And walk forever in the path of truth,
A servant yet a son; a sire and yet a youth.

Is not that taking Jesus as the author of the *Imitation* took him?

Very has been several times compared to George Herbert; but the comparison does not seem to me apt. They both were what are called 'religious poets,' to be sure. So was Watts. Very, moreover, has an occasional line in the manner of Herbert, as:

Then hast me fenced about with thorny talk.

But Herbert was an epigrammatist, I had almost said a wit; at any rate an Elizabethan, as full of conceits and word-plays as Shakespeare or Chapman himself. To compare him with Emerson would be juster. Very is the farthest possible removed from conceits of any kind. He is no Elizabethan of the seventeenth century, but rather suggests an Italian or a German of the thirteenth, one of the divine race to which belonged the author of the *Imitation*.

In this first part of the poems, as, indeed, in all of them, there comes out the strenuous insistence on the submission of the will to God, submission in itself inevitable, but a source of the highest joy, if made voluntarily. The idea is not new. Have we not Epictetus saying to us: 'But to be instructed is this: to learn to wish that everything may happen as it does. And how do things happen? As the Disposer has disposed them.' And again, often and often in the Christian world comes the same refrain, filled, it cannot be denied, with a light and radiance which it lacked with Epictetus. But in the last century, the world has certainly not heard it as often as before, and we in America cannot be said to have heard it oftener than the rest of the world. Hence it seems to me very valuable, as it comes to us in these poems, and because here it is rested perhaps on a larger basis than in more perfectly Christian ages of the world.

In 'The Message' we find collected sonnets which deal, for the most part, with Very's performance of his mission in rebuke and appeal to other men. I do not think that his highest claim to consideration lies in this; but perhaps it is the most original point in him, the point least to be paralleled in the literature of which he forms a part. Emerson, to be sure, exhorts, encourages, instructs; but the tone of Very is different. There is a certain sternness in it, a flavor of absolutism, which carries one back a thousand, two thousand years, out of modern skepticism and doubt where men at best do no more than find conviction for themselves. 'He spoke as one having authority, and not as the Scribes and Pharisees.'

JONES VERY

'Tis to yourself I speak; you cannot know
Him whom I call in speaking such a one.
For you beneath the earth lie buried low,
Which he alone, as living, walks upon.
You may at times have heard him speak to you,
And often wished perchance that you were he;
And I must ever wish that it were true
For then you could hold fellowship with me:

Go, cleanse thy lying mouth of all its guile
That from the will within thee ever flows;
Go, cleanse the temple thou dost now defile.
Then shall I cease to feel thy heavy blows;
And come and tread with me the path of peace,
And from thy brother's harm forever cease.

It is Emerson who compares Very to David and
Isaiah. In this point of his character the comparison is just. By his passionate sensibility to
Nature, by his broad and spiritual view of God, he
stands apart from them; but he has in common
with them, if in a far less degree, that authority
and prophetic sternness, that austerity and severity of purpose, which laid the scourge again and
again on the backs of the wayward and disobedient
Jews. And he has also, in common with them, a
sense of wrath and scorn at the meanness and
pettiness of men around him, a feeling of isolation
in the midst of a people who have fallen off from
God.

My heart grows sick before the wide-spread death
That walks and speaks in seeming life around;
And I would love the corpse without a breath
That sleeps forgotten 'neath the cold, cold ground.

See also the sonnet entitled 'Faith,' and the one beginning:

> There is no worship now: the idol stands
> Within the Spirit's holy resting-place!

And especially the one following:

> I have no brother. They who meet me now
> Offer a hand with their own wills defiled.

Is it not the same desolate cry which comes always from the inspired lips: 'He came unto his own and his own received him not'? And not from the saints only, but from the poet and from the sage, every man who sees without the emptiness and folly and frivolity of the world, and within the intense reality of things. It is by this chord that Very is in sympathy with many men of his century who are otherwise so different from him, men like Shelley and Leopardi; or the strange and forlorn author of *Obermann*, men bound together, not by beliefs or creeds, but by a common hatred of the meanness and pretension by which so many souls are chained, men who stand side by side regardless of their differences:

> The children of the second birth
> Whom the world could not tame.

But let us turn to a calmer page. One must not look too long and too deeply into these things, else we also might perchance grow mad. After man let us take Nature. It is the refuge which many a weary heart has sought before us, and many more will seek it after. I know few better guides to it than Very. Not that he is one of the great word-painters. He does not show us the external world in a rich, sensuous glamour like Keats, nor does he idealize it into a dream like Shelley, nor clothe it in purple, sunset splendor, like Byron. His rendering of it is more that of Wordsworth, a seizing of delicate points and making them stand out before the eye almost unobscured by the veil of language; but Wordsworth at his best moments has far more inspiration than Very, more illumination, if I may use the word; and at his worst he has far less sympathy. This is what makes Very so singular and so precious: his identification of himself with Nature, his losing himself in pure adoration. He forgets to write for the sake of writing, but lets his feelings flow directly from his pen.

> Nature! my love for thee is deeper far
> Than strength of words, though spirit-born, can tell;
> For while I gaze they seem my soul to bar,
> That in thy widening streams would onward swell,
> Bearing thy mirrored beauty on its breast.

This figure of a river seems especially to charm him. He turns to it again and again, delighting himself with the calmness of it:

> A motion that scarce knows itself from rest.
> Amid the fields I am a child again,
> The spots that then I loved, I love the more,
> My fingers drop the strangely-scrawling pen
> And I remember nought but Nature's lore.

'Strangely-scrawling pen' is somewhat forced, but
we can feel the note. The group of sonnets called
'Nature' is all in this strain. I wish I could quote
largely from it; but the reader must examine for
himself. I can hardly do more than mention the
names. Take, for instance, the sonnet entitled
'The Spirit':

> I would not breathe, when blows thy mighty wind
> O'er desolate hill and winter-blasted plain.

Could one catch better the mighty sweep of a No-
vember gale? And everywhere Nature is touched
and lighted up by the presence of the soul. Seeing
the snow which covers and purifies all, he hears
man bid it cover his heart also:

> But all in vain: its guilt can never hide
> From the quick Spirit's heart-deep searching eye;
> The barren plains and caverns yawning wide
> Lie ever naked to the passer-by;
> Nor can one thought deformed the presence shun,
> But to the Spirit's gaze stands bright as in the sun.

Read 'The Violet':

> The nearest neighbor of the creeping vines.

In such lines as that one sees Very's best vein. No
splendor of Miltonic inversion, no sublimity; a
feeling moulding its own words, and admirable
simplicity. Simplicity! We hear of it often nowadays. I am a little weary of the phrase myself. We
forget so readily that between simplicity and commonplace there is an immense gulf fixed.

JONES VERY

A word or two more about the division 'Nature,' and then we will pass on. I spoke a little while ago of Very's entire identification of himself with Nature. The phrase is something overworn; but in his case it had reality. With him it means far more than an after-dinner admiration of rainbows and the sunset glow, more even than a careful study of Nature and a poetical interpretation of her. There are minutes when he seems to enter into her being, to breathe her breath, to throb, himself, with that mysterious life which we have all of us, at minutes, a faint intuition of, but which few, it seems to me, have felt as he did. At least few have given such utterance to that feeling of it. One sonnet, that to 'The Columbine,' is especially noticeable for this:

> Still, still, my eye will gaze long-fixed on thee
> Till I forget that I am called a man,
> And at thy side fast-rooted seem to be,
> And the breeze comes my cheek with thine to fan.
> Upon this craggy hill our life shall pass, —
> A life of summer days and summer joys, —
> Nodding our honey-bells 'mid pliant grass
> In which the bee, half-hid, his time employs;
> And here we'll drink with thirsty pores the rain,
> And turn, dew-sprinkled, to the rising sun,
> And look when in the flaming west again
> His orb across the heaven its path has run;
> Here left in darkness on the rocky steep,
> My weary eyes shall close like folding flowers in sleep.

Nodding our honey-bells 'mid pliant grass
In which the bee, half-hid, his time employs.

JONES VERY

Could Keats himself have given better the intense yet indolent existence of it all? Nature! The calm, the undisturbed One! Ah, if one could go to her sometimes, away from this wearisome, bustling external life! Most of us cannot. We know not how. And this strain of Very's comes to us like a breath from an open window in spring afternoons, when the dampness is curling up from the earth, and one is grown so tired of winter and of storm.

I must delay here no longer. Let me just refer in passing to 'The Sabbatia,' 'The Canary Bird,' 'The Trees of Life.' Observe also, in 'The Barberry Bush,' the momentary recurrence to a strain of anger at the perversity of men.

All the sonnets in this section 'Nature' are interesting. One finds an occasional awkwardness and carelessness of expression; but the average is Very's best. Just the reverse is the case with the division entitled 'Song and Praise.' One finds there some of his weakest work, and, side by side with it, some of his greatest. Take, for instance, the following:

> The comings on of Faith,
> The goings out of Sight,
> Are as the brightening of the morn,
> And dying of the night.

And again, in another strain:

> For thy return in vain shall wait
> Thy tender young, thy fond, fond mate,
> Till night's last stars beam forth full late
> On their sad eyes,
> Unknown, alas, thy cruel fate,
> Unheard thy cries.

JONES VERY

Take with these 'The Prayer' at the beginning, 'The Fossil Flower,' the 'Lines to —— on the Death of His Friend' — there are few things in the whole book finer than these. But on the other side, we have 'The Tenant' and 'The Sight of the Ocean':

> I turned from the dark and rocky height,
> With grateful heart to my hearthstone bright.

That recalls Wordsworth in his bathetic fits, or I do not know what hymns of our childhood. Here again one sees his lack of literary skill. The truth is, Very wrote wholly by his inspiration. When that failed him, he had no talent to keep him up, and he wrote very poor stuff indeed.

The book closes with eight or ten sonnets collected under the title of 'The Beginning and the End.' Over these we must pause an instant; for they will repay our pains. All of them, I think, are worthy of their author: they have hardly any of his characteristic weaknesses. Indeed, it seems as if the Shakespearian sonnet were Very's true instrument. In that he is at home, and can do what he will. With other lyrical forms he cannot feel at ease.

Two or three extracts I shall make here, the last; but without them, this sketch could not be complete. They are entitled 'Love' and 'Beauty'; and in reading them one is reminded for a moment of the exquisite hymns of Spenser which go by the same name. Indeed, if one thinks of it, there is a certain relation between these two: a bond of purity, and, as it were, celestial grace, which unites the

younger to the elder and greater genius. But to
return. The first of these sonnets, that on 'Love,'
runs thus:

> I asked of Time to tell me where was Love:
> He pointed to her footsteps on the snow,
> Where first the angel lighted from above,
> And bid me note the way and onward go,
> Through populous streets of cities spreading wide,
> By lonely cottage rising on the moor,
> Where bursts from sundered cliff the struggling tide,
> To where it hails the sea with answering roar,
> She led me on; o'er mountain's frozen head,
> Where mile on mile still stretches on the plain,
> Then homeward whither first my feet she led,
> I traced her path along the snow again;
> But there the sun had melted from the earth
> The prints where first she trod, a child of mortal birth.

It makes one pause a little over the allegory; but
see the next. There is an evident progression between the three.

> Thy beauty fades, and with it, too, my love;
> For 'twas the self-same stock that bore its flower.
> Soft fell the rain, and, breaking from above,
> The sun looked out upon our nuptial hour;
> And I had thought forever by thy side
> With bursting buds of hope in youth to dwell,
> But one by one Time strewed thy petals wide,
> And every hope's wan look a grief can tell;
> For I had thoughtless lived beneath his sway,
> Who like a tyrant dealeth with us all,
> Crowning each rose, though rooted on decay,
> With charms that shall the Spirit's love enthrall,
> And for a season turn the soul's pure eyes
> From virtue's changeless bloom that time and death defies.

Is not that perfect Spenser, that last lengthened line, the Alexandrine? But let me give one more, by far the most perfect of the three, and then I have done. Notice, moreover, in this the second quatrain. I know few things more passionate in English literature. Certainly it is far more so than anything else of Very's. Whether the sonnet has any biographical value or not, I do not know.

> I gazed upon thy face, — and beating life
> Once stilled its sleepless pulses in my breast,
> And every thought whose being was a strife,
> Each in its silent chamber sank to rest.
> I was not, save it were a thought of thee;
> The world was but a spot where thou had'st trod;
> From every star thy glance seemed fixed on me;
> Almost I loved thee better than my God.
> And still I gaze, — but 'tis a holier thought
> Than that which in my spirit lived before,
> Each star a purer ray of love has caught,
> Earth wears a lovelier robe than then it wore,
> And every lamp that burns around thy shrine
> Is fed with fire whose fountain is divine.

Do you see the Eros peeping out there, like a child's face in a green wall of ivy, frightened, and drawing back again a minute after? Conscience and calmer thought will not tolerate him. We must not love anything but God.

So it ends as it began, with the love of God. 'I am Alpha and Omega, the beginning and the end.' Unfortunately, most of us nowadays have no time to think about that.

I shall be asked why I have dwelt thus long on a

man so little known as Jones Very. To be sure, he is not and never can be one of the great figures in literature. His breadth is not sufficiently great in proportion to his depth. Moreover, the outward forms of current religious phraseology, in which he clothed his profound spiritual life, are to a certain degree repulsive to many men of this generation; and on the other hand, his passionate idealism does not altogether please comfortable orthodoxy. Yet I cannot help thinking that there are two points in Very, which ought to give him a place, permanent, at least, if not prominent, in our literature: his love of Nature and his mysticism. I know well that with our vast material civilization the love of Nature and mysticism have little to do. Yet I, myself, have a belief, perhaps unwarranted, in certain deeper sides of human nature, which makes me think that one day our vast material civilization, as it at present exists, may be all gone —

Like what seemed corporal, melted into thin air;

and then the world may be inclined to find a small place even for such men as Jones Very.

Be that as it may, I, at least, moved by the delight I have received from Very, have been led to bring such a tribute as was in my power to his name, a name, certainly, not of the greatest, and yet, as it seems to me, a name which ought not to be forgotten.

VIII
THE LETTERS OF HORACE WALPOLE

CHRONOLOGY

HORACE WALPOLE, FOURTH EARL OF ORFORD

Born, London, September 24, 1717 (O.S.).

At King's College, Cambridge, 1735–39.

Toured Europe with Thomas Gray, 1739–41.

In Parliament, 1741–68.

Purchased place near Twickenham and named it Strawberry Hill, 1748. (He had leased it in 1747.)

Established private printing-press at Strawberry Hill,
July, 1757.

The Castle of Otranto published, 1764.

Visited Paris and formed friendship with Mme. du Deffand,
1765.

Succeeded to Earldom of Orford on the death of his nephew
the third Earl, 1791.

Died, Berkeley Square, London, March 2, 1797.

VIII

THE LETTERS OF HORACE WALPOLE

OF MAKING many editions of letters there is no end. You purchase something which purports to be elaborate, complete, and final, and before you are well at home in it, another collection succeeds, revised, enlarged, and enriched with curious material, rescued from old garrets and worm-eaten trunks, where it has lain for years, unprized and unregarded. In this fashion the enormous correspondence of Voltaire has grown and grown, until it has come to include over ten thousand letters; and as new documents constantly turn up, one asks one's self in despair whether he is not still dispatching them from his present abode — an idea not wholly lacking in piquancy.

Walpole's correspondence is less extensive than Voltaire's. But, by a similar process, it has developed from a modest volume or so in the first edition of Lord Orford's works, through three volumes, and four volumes, and six volumes, to nine large volumes collected by Cunningham in 1857, and now to sixteen volumes carefully edited and elaborately annotated by Mrs. Paget Toynbee. Yet even this immense work does not contain all the material known to exist, since Mrs. Toynbee informs us that a certain number of unpublished original letters of Walpole are in the possession of the Earl of Ilchester, who 'was unable to accede to my request for permission to include these letters in the present edition.' Family reasons may naturally account for this refusal, but if it is the result of a collector's selfishness, it is not especially creditable to his lordship.

What Mrs. Toynbee has omitted is, however, of no consequence, when we consider what she has been able to add. Cunningham printed 2654 letters. Mrs. Toynbee prints 3061, 111 for the first time. Much of this new material is, of course, comparatively uninteresting, brief notes on business or family affairs, yet even these are often important for the study of Walpole's character, as showing his nicety of feeling in money matters and his constant devotion to the interests of his friends; while the French letters to Madame du Deffand are in the highest degree valuable in connection with that lady's brilliant and characteristic correspondence; and the extensive series to Lady Mary Coke and that to Miss Anne Pitt, already printed, but now first collected, are in Walpole's easiest, sprightliest vein, and will afford endless delight to all lovers of the master of Strawberry Hill.

Mrs. Toynbee has done her author good service in other ways besides the collection of new letters. She has made many alterations in the chronology of Cunningham's arrangement, which was a careful piece of work for its day, but left room for a great deal of improvement. She has also much amended the text, especially of the letters to Mann, restoring numerous passages which Cunningham omitted without comment. For instance, letter 2183 (edition Toynbee) is nearly three times as long as its equivalent in Cunningham, although in this case the editor has not troubled herself to call attention to the fact.

On the difficult point of annotation, Mrs. Toynbee's work is, for the most part, satisfactory. In biographical details, dates, and the like, she has made a very great advance on former editions. One could wish, however, that she had been a little freer with the sort of accessory information which is all the more delightful for not being absolutely indispensable. Lack of space would naturally restrain her from supplying the abundant feast of erudition which lends such charm to Mr. Tovey's *Letters of Thomas Gray*, but it seems a pity not to have retained more of the curious gossip so painstakingly accumulated by Dover, Wright, and the rest. These, however, are minor matters. From every point of view Mrs. Paget Toynbee has done a monumental piece of work, creditable in the highest degree for accuracy and thoroughness, and certain to be of the greatest value to every future student of English history in the eighteenth century.*

* In the following analysis of Walpole's character and correspondence I have drawn my quotations, as far as possible, from the material either first printed or first collected by Mrs. Paget Toynbee, and the extent to which I have been able to do this shows the importance of the work done by her.

THE LETTERS OF HORACE WALPOLE

Horace Walpole, the youngest son of the great minister, Sir Robert Walpole, was born in the year 1717. Educated at Eton and Cambridge, he early became intimately acquainted with some of the foremost literary men of his time. His situation of course afforded him every opportunity for political distinction, and for many years he was a member of the House of Commons and personally familiar with all the great Parliamentary leaders, but he never took any prominent share in public affairs, and during the latter part of his long life he chose to observe and criticize rather than to act. He was always a dabbler in literature, though disclaiming any serious ambitions for authorship. His *Catalogue of Royal and Noble Authors, Anecdotes of Painting,* and *Historic Doubts on the Life and Reign of King Richard the Third* gave him a certain standing as a critic and historian. *The Mysterious Mother*, a tragedy, was highly praised by Byron, though Walpole himself called it 'disgusting from the subject and totally unfit for the stage.' *The Castle of Otranto* is interesting as the first work of the great school of romantic fiction which astonished the earlier part of the nineteenth century with its productions, and has had such a vigorous revival in recent years. Walpole's specimen is no worse than many of the others, and shares with most of them the disadvantage of existing apparently for the sole purpose of showing the superiority of Scott. Walpole also wrote historical memoirs of his own time, not remarkable

218

for either accuracy or picturesqueness. When he was seventy-four years old, he succeeded his nephew in the earldom of Orford, which had been created for Sir Robert, but this new dignity brought Walpole little advantage or satisfaction. He died in 1797, after watching with melancholy foreboding the horrors of the French Revolution.

Certainly, none of the writings above referred to would have sufficed to keep Walpole's name alive as anything more than a literary curiosity. But during the whole of his long career he was an active and unwearying letter-writer, and the vast accumulation of his correspondence constitutes a monument of which any author might well be proud. To be sure, Walpole's letters are always literary, conscious, to a certain extent artificial. At eighteen years of age we find him writing to his friend Montagu: 'You have made me a very unreasonable request, which I will answer with another as extraordinary: you desire I would burn your letters, I desire you would keep mine.' If this was his frame of mind at eighteen, it is not likely to have altered at eighty. Therefore we must not look in Walpole for the instantaneous self-photography which makes the charm of the correspondence of Cicero, nor for the absolute simplicity and naturalness of Cowper or of Edward Fitzgerald.

Madame de Sévigné suggests a more suitable comparison. That Walpole tried to model his letter-writing upon that famous lady's is more than probable. His enthusiastic admiration of her was expressed at every period of his life. 'You have undone yourself with me, for you compare them [his letters] to Madame de Sévigné's; absolute treason! Do you know, there is scarce a book in the world I love so much as her letters?' Again, he speaks of buying 'the portrait that was Madame de Simiane's'; 'I am going to build an altar for it under the title of *Notre Dame des Rochers*.' Also, he must surely have had Madame de Sévigné in mind when he declared that women are better letter-writers than men; 'for our sex is too jealous of the reputation of good sense to hazard a thousand trifles and negligences which give grace, ease, and familiarity to correspondence.'

Walpole himself was always sufficiently jealous of his reputation for good sense, yet, assuredly, no woman ever hazarded more trifles and negligences. Hazarded is hardly the word, however. Madame de Sévigné may have hazarded such things. Walpole hunts for them, gloats over them, piles them up. So, being but a clumsy male, after all, he misses much of the 'grace, ease, and familiarity' which give 'Our Lady of the Rocks' such immortal freshness and charm. Only, Walpole had no daughter, and in this he had distinctly the advantage of his French model.

What one looks for first in correspondence is the writer himself. Even the student, whose final object is historical facts or social pictures, must begin by observing the transmitting medium, that is, the painting and recording mind. A man cannot write letters every week or oftener, for sixty years, to scores of correspondents, without leaving a likeness of himself, more perfect and minute than was ever sketched by Rembrandt or Velasquez. Unfortunately, the portrait of Walpole has not usually been found very pleasing. Indeed, Macaulay, as is well known, in his incisive fashion labeled the author of the letters as an idler, an affected fop, socially a snob, politically a sneering indifferentist, and morally a cynical *pococurante*.

Allowing for Macaulay's 'heightened and telling way of putting things,' it would be difficult to deny that there is some truth in these charges. Walpole avoided the strenuous, on principle. He shunned ambition, large activities, and preferred the lighter pursuits, which, if less stimulating, are also less deceptive. His was the epigrammatic saying which may now be read on the advertisements of a popular specific: 'Life is a comedy to those who think, a tragedy to those who feel.' Being inclined by nature rather to thinking than to feeling, he set himself to develop this inborn tendency, and had a good measure of success.

The passion for political distinction he early and completely laid aside. 'My books, my *virtu*, and my other follies and amusements take up too much of my time to leave me much leisure to think of other people's affairs; and of all affairs, those of the public are least my concern.' So he wrote in his youth, and the note in his old age was the same:

'I will never think on politics more. What has a man to do with them, who never felt a titillation of ambition?'

The passion for literature was never more to him than a whim or fancy, which was, doubtless, the reason why his literary work was never anything more than whimsical or fanciful. In his heart of hearts he had the feeling, always so common in England, that writing is an occupation unworthy of a gentleman. 'What is the merit of a mere man of letters?' 'You know I have always thought a running footman as meritorious a being as a learned man.'

In the common relations of life he was equally averse to any intensity of emotion. At twenty-four years of age he wrote, 'I am neither young enough nor old enough to be in love.' Apparently he never got to be old enough — nor young enough. He never married, and when Madame du Deffand, nearly seventy years old, and more than a score of years older than he, conceived for him that singular passion which was the crowning grace of a singular life, his response to it was marked much more by the fear of ridicule than by the ardor of affection. With friendship it was the same. '*Though I don't love loving*, I could have poured out all the fullness of my heart to such an old and true friend,' he writes to George Montagu; and to Lady Mary Coke: 'You must not give way to all the friendship you are capable of. By some means or other it will embitter your whole life; and though it is very insipid to be indifferent, the vexations consequential of attachments are much too dearly bought by any satisfaction they produce.' It might be thought that a man of this temper would at least love nature. Listen to him: 'I hate the country: I am past the shepherdly age of groves and streams, and am not arrived at that of hating everything but what I do myself, as building and planting.' Yet he hastens to tell us that this distaste for natural pleasures does not arrive from any overfondness for society: 'I am so far from growing used to mankind by living amongst them, that my natural ferocity and wildness does but every day grow worse. They tire me, they fatigue me; I don't know what to do with them; I don't know what to say to them; I fling open the windows and fancy I want air; and when I get by myself, I undress myself, and seem to have had people in my pockets, in my plaits, and on my shoulders.'

The sum of the whole matter is, that life taken seriously is intolerable. '*Il faut glisser sur les pensées,*' says 'Our Lady of the Rocks,' '*et ne pas les approfondir.*' Live on the surface. Play with trifles which amuse and neither deceive nor entangle. 'This world is one great Alas! Most men suffer, yet all extol their chief plagues.' If we would drown the groans and stifle the yawns, let us keep Folly's bells a-jangling — 'Folly, the cordial drop that Heaven in our cup has thrown.'

A prophet, this, not likely to appeal to an age of

strenuousness, like ours, an age overburdened with the seriousness of life and perhaps also, just a little, with its own importance. Yet there were worse men than Walpole in his own day, and there are worse now.

For his disinterestedness in money matters we have his own word, and I think we may accept it — with other evidence. 'Thank you for your Exchequer-ward wishes for me,' he writes to George Montagu, 'but I am apt to think that I have enough from thence already — don't think my horns and hoofs are growing when I profess indifference to my interest. Disinterestedness is no merit in me; it happens to be my passion.'

Theoretical disclaimers of friendship often go hand in hand with devoted attachments, and, though extreme devotion was hardly in Walpole's nature, it is impossible to doubt that he sincerely loved a few persons who were near to him. It would be difficult to improve on his attitude toward his father. 'A son who adores his father,' he calls himself; and on the numerous occasions which arise for defending Sir Robert's memory, he acquits himself always with tact and dignity. Nor can we question his genuine affection for Conway, for Montagu, for Chute, for Mann, an affection which even sometimes manifested itself in actions. His reception of Madame du Deffand's caresses may not have been always sympathetic during her life; but his words, when she was on her deathbed, have every mark of sincere grief: 'Should she be capable of hearing it, when you receive this, I entreat you to tell her — but I do not know how to express how much I love her and how much I feel.'

Macaulay is very bitter about Walpole's politics, accusing him of hypocritically praising liberty, while remaining at heart a thorough aristocrat; but who of us is really in a position to throw stones at such an inconsistency as this? I do not in the least doubt that Walpole loved liberty and would even have made some — not excessive — sacrifices for it. When he says, 'The spirit of liberty alone has made me at any time attend to them [politics]; for life without freedom has but a narrower or a wider prison,' I believe he means as much as nine tenths of those who have uttered similar sentiments — Macaulay not excepted. On a more tangible ground, that of humanity, Walpole is still more worthy of admiration. During the whole of his long life, like a true son of his father, he raised his voice unfalteringly against the stupid wickedness of war and the barrenness of military glory. There are still a few persons by whom this will be counted unto him for righteousness. The following somewhat lengthy passage is well worth quoting for the credit of that age and the benefit of this: 'We cannot live without destroying animals, but shall we torture them for our sport, sport in their destruction? I met a rough officer at his house t'other day, who said he knew such a person was turning Methodist, for, in the middle of conversation, he rose and opened the window to let out a moth. I told him I did not know the Methodists had any principle so good, and that I, who am certainly not on the point of becoming one, always did so too. One of the bravest and best men I ever knew, Sir Charles Wager, I have often heard declare he never killed a fly willingly. It is a comfortable reflection to me that all the victories of last year have been gained since the suppression of the Bear Garden and prize-fighting; as it is plain, and nothing else would have made it so, that our valour did not singly and solely depend upon these two Universities.'

Lastly, we, on this side of the Atlantic, should have some tenderness for Walpole, because he sympathized very little with the tyrannical methods of George the Third, and because of his enthusiastic prophecies as to our future. 'You have seen the accounts from Boston. The tocsin seems to be sounded in America. I have many visions about that country and fancy I see twenty empires and republics forming upon vast scales over all that continent, which is growing too mighty to be kept in subjection to half a dozen exhausted nations in Europe.'

But, after all, the man in Walpole's letters interests us less than the powerful painter of the times. Pepys had more vividness and more genuineness than his successor. Saint-Simon had more passion and more genius. But Pepys's vision was slow and limited, and Saint-Simon's was obscured by his fantastic hobbies. Walpole touched everything, saw everything, heard everything, recorded everything. If we want grand, historic scenes, what can satisfy us better than the trial of the rebel lords or the burial of George the Second? If we want lifelike pictures of statesmen and orators, which of these volumes does not abound in them? It is true, Macaulay charges Walpole with systematic depreciation of all the greatest men of his age, and the charge cannot be wholly refuted. A satirist and a contemporary, who sees the hero without his robes and laurels, is always too prone to insist upon details which posterity would willingly forget. Chatham, the greatest hero of all, is too frequently the object of Walpole's unkindly comment; yet, for that very reason, what intense sincerity do we feel in this glowing account of his oratory: 'He spoke at past one, for an hour and thirty-five minutes; there was more humor, wit, vivacity, finer language, more boldness, in short, more astonishing perfections than even you, who are used to him, can conceive.'

When we turn to lesser men, whom we are not so accustomed to imagining upon a pedestal, Walpole's portraits have an extraordinary and fascinating vivacity and brilliancy. For instance, Mrs. Paget Toynbee, in a hitherto unprinted letter, gives us this sketch of the versatile Charles Townshend, whose willful short-sightedness was so important an element in bringing on the American Revolution: 'Charles Townshend has entertained us with another interlude: took part against Lord

Chatham; declared himself out of place, nobody knew whether turned out or resigning; kept away on a great day of his own business; hatched a quarrel with Colonel Barré; returned yesterday to the House; acted as Chancellor of the Exchequer; outwent the rest of the ministers; made no mention of Barré; talked of his measures for the rest of the session; and probably dines with Lord Rockingham today and sups with the Duke of Grafton. What he will do next, besides exposing himself, you, nor I, nor he can tell.'

And in a memorandum found among Miss Berry's papers and now first printed, Walpole gives us another vivid glimpse of the same eccentric personage, addressing the House of Commons, when he was half-drunk: 'In this speech he beat Lord Chatham in language, Burke in metaphors, Grenville in presumption, Rigby in impudence, himself in folly, and everybody in good-humor, for he pleased while he provoked at random; was malicious to nobody, cheerful to all; and if his speech was received with delight, it was only remembered with pity.'

Of all the figures so satirically sketched by Walpole none is more striking than that of the Duke of Newcastle. A cunning flatterer, a juggling schemer, a prince of corruption in the most corrupt of ages, a clown, a mountebank, at times almost a driveling idiot — we should certainly conclude that this fantastic caricature was the mere invention of Walpole's personal hatred, if we did not find Lord Hervey confirming it in language which the *Atlantic* could not possibly print. How immense is the power of these memoir- and letter-writers, when with a few deft turns of the pen they can create or mar a reputation, can pose a character before posterity in any attitude they please, can overcome the sober testimony of fact, and impress their own love and hatred on the memory of mankind to endless generations! What statesman of today, glorious in the flattery of his contemporaries, petted and spoiled by the press and the place-hunter, but would shudder to think of himself dancing forever in naked ignominy before the ages, like the Duke of Newcastle at the funeral of George the Second?

'This grave scene was fully contrasted by the burlesque Duke of Newcastle. He fell into a fit of crying the moment he came into the chapel, and flung himself back in a stall, the Archbishop hovering over him with a smelling-bottle — but in two minutes his curiosity got the better of his hypocrisy, and he ran about the chapel, with his glass, to spy who was or was not there, spying with one hand and mopping his eyes with t'other. Then returned the fear of catching cold, and the Duke of Cumberland, who was sinking with heat, felt himself weighed down, and found it was the Duke of Newcastle, standing upon his train to avoid the chill of the marble.'

Walpole's literary gossip is less interesting than his political. As regards taste in general he is fairly

229

representative of his contemporaries, although leaning somewhat toward innovation. The strange, the romantic, the picturesque, tempted him, filled him with a sort of timid joy. *The Castle of Otranto* is pseudo-mediæval, and Strawberry Hill was pseudo-Gothic; but the author of both was really more comfortable in the trimmed and finished surroundings of his own eighteenth century. There was genuine English stuff in him somewhere, however. Again and again he proclaims his enthusiasm for Shakespeare; and one of the most interesting of the letters newly collected by Mrs. Paget Toynbee is that to Jephson which speaks of certain Shakespearean passages as 'texts out of the book of nature, in comparison of which the works of all other writers in every language that I understand are to me apocryphal.'

To the authors of his own time, as men, Walpole is generally indifferent, as one would expect from what I quoted above about his contempt for the literary profession, and from his remark as to the youthful Burke: 'a sensible man, but has not worn off his authorism yet, and thinks there is nothing so charming as writers, and to be one. He will know better one of these days.' Gray, Walpole first patronized, then quarreled with, then flattered. His conduct to Chatterton was long considered to have been cruel and heartless, and although these adjectives are probably too strong, there was much in it to be regretted, much which Walpole himself regretted at a later period of his life. His comments on the great French writers, whom he knew more or less intimately, are usually slighting and depreciative. Of Voltaire, for instance, he says that he was 'as mean and dirty as he was envious.' As for literary personages against whom he had a political or social grudge, he loses no opportunity of presenting them in an odious or ridiculous light. He can never say enough of the objectionable eccentricities of Lady Mary Montagu, and he abuses Dr. Johnson as savagely as Dr. Johnson would probably have abused him: 'The saucy Caliban'; 'the tasteless pedant'; 'Dr. Johnson has indubitably neither taste nor ear, [nor any] criterion of judgment but his old woman's prejudices.'

Two books, which were immensely popular in their own day and have ever since ranked among the greatest productions of English literature, receive from Walpole a severe condemnation. *Clarissa Harlowe* he calls 'a picture of high life as conceived by a bookseller, and a romance as it would be spiritualized by a Methodist teacher.' Of Sterne's masterpiece he says: 'At present nothing is talked of, nothing admired, but what I cannot help calling a very insipid and tedious performance ... the great humor of which consists in the whole narrative always going backwards.... It makes one smile two or three times at the beginning, but in recompense makes one yawn for two hours.'

The most characteristic feature of Walpole's correspondence is, undoubtedly, the picture of the social world in which he lived. He was intimately acquainted with the best society of his day in both England and France, and that society was something which had never been seen before and may never be seen again. The crudeness of the seventeenth century had worn off, and the vast cosmopolitanism of the nineteenth had not yet obliterated that personal feature which must always be the most vital element of conversation. The grace, the ease, the vivacity, the courtly polish, the ready wit, of George Selwyn and Gilly Williams, of Madame du Deffand and Madame de Choiseul, and of scores of others like them — all this is too delicate and evanescent in its charm ever to be perfectly conveyed to us by the dull medium of ink and paper. Yet we are grateful for even a dim reflection of a world so fascinating.

Anyone who wishes to come as nearly as possible into direct contact with this eighteenth-century life will do well to look through Jesse's *George Selwyn and his Contemporaries*. There, in the carefully preserved correspondence of a man who was himself one of the central social figures of his time, we have the actual letters of men and women of birth, breeding, and wit, who open their hearts to us without a thought of attitudinizing or literary effect. It is one of the most significant and striking records of genuine human nature that exist.

Few men could be better qualified to be the literary reporter of this brilliant period than Horace Walpole. His curiosity was, indeed, less passionate than Saint-Simon's; but perhaps it was

all the better suited to a more frivolous age. And,
though not passionate, Walpole's curiosity was
ever present. If he did not love humanity, he was
always interested in it, in all its moods and phases.
He studied the complex motives of great statesmen,
which stirred three or four continents, and it
amused him to see that those motives were sometimes as great as the men and sometimes of a pettiness all the more astonishing for the mass of the
results that flowed from them. It was, in part, this
pettiness which made him so alive to the trifles
that called forth Macaulay's buskined rhetoric —
trifles oftentimes important because significant of
human life and human character. The wafting of
a billet-doux, the flutter of a fan, the new fashion
of a garment, the chatter of gay youths about a
card-table, the elopement of a beauty, a duel, a
robbery on the highway, an odd funeral, or a brilliant wedding — all these thin and glittering
threads which make up the tissue of common existence — how deftly Walpole twists and turns and
disentangles them!

Now it is a day at Strawberry Hill, 'the puppet
show of the time.' Walpole does the honors to a
group of French and English ladies, under the
leadership of the Duchess of Grafton, 'who perfectly entered into the air of enchantment and
fairyism, which is the tone of the place.' Or he
visits Esher with the same company: 'I never
passed a more agreeable day than yesterday.... It
was Parnassus, as Watteau would have painted it.'

THE LETTERS OF HORACE WALPOLE

Now it is Vauxhall, with its more mixed company, its crowds, and gayety; or Ranelagh, with the 'vast amphitheatre, finely gilt, painted, and illuminated, into which everybody that loves eating, drinking, staring, or crowding, is admitted for twelvepence.'

Now it is cards, but Walpole is no great friend to them. Then, as today, they were a substitute for conversation, and were its worst enemy, whist especially, which 'has spread an universal opium over the whole nation; it makes courtiers and patriots sit down to the same pack of cards.' And our chronicler again and again refers to the gambling fever which, hand in hand with cards, had taken possession of every order of society. 'We have the most delightful of all summers — fruit, flowers, corn, grass, leaves — in short, though Judæa flowed with milk and honey, I do not believe it was much richer than the present face of England. I know of but one richer spot, which is Almack's, where a thousand meadows and cornfields are staked at every throw, and as many villages lost as in the earthquake that overwhelmed Herculaneum and Pompeii.'

So the gay and the rich and the careless trifled away the time. And because, after all, their life, charming as it was, was lived only for themselves, only for trifles, those among them who really thought were always on the verge of deadly ennui. Madame du Deffand, the noble heart, the serious intellect, found herself bored from youth to age.

THE LETTERS OF HORACE WALPOLE

Even Walpole, who had a gift for distraction, cried out in his early days, 'One can't pass one's youth too amusingly; for one must grow old, and that in England; two most serious circumstances, either of which makes people gray in the twinkling of a bedstaff.' And forty years later comes the quiet comment, 'Nothing can be more insipid than my life.'

Yes, they thought only of themselves, of their own society, their own order, these brilliant, charming ladies, these gay, witty, courtly gentlemen. The narrow world in which they lived was to them the sole possible world, the best world. They had no idea of the stupendous changes which were so soon to come, of the new heaven and the new earth which were to take the place of their pleasant dalliance and graceful vanities. Walpole lived through the French Revolution; but the impression of it in his correspondence is only one of horror. He was a liberal, but after the stiffly conservative fashion of English liberalism. From the first volume to the last, his letters are eighteenth century and nothing but eighteenth century. He would have been out of sympathy not only with the politics of the age which followed, its democracy, its humanitarianism, but with all its dreamy desires, its vast and vague aspirings, its spiritual agony, its passionate hope. One wonders — or no, one knows — what Walpole would have thought of the poetry of Shelley, of the music of Beethoven, of the philosophy of Hegel.

IX
BIOGRAPHY BY MIRROR

IX
BIOGRAPHY BY MIRROR

I

WITH the basis of biography solidly established in the common identity of the human heart, we will give the next few pages to considering some of the elements, some forms of the raw material, of which biography is composed, these elements naturally dealing with various manifestations of the fundamental basis.

The first of these elements that suggests itself is the formal effort of men and women to describe their own lives in autobiography. In a large room of the Uffizi Gallery in Florence are gathered together a group of portraits of great painters, painted by themselves from their reflections in the glass. These portraits are full of significance and rich suggestion for the lives and characters of the painters. At the same time there is usually a certain suggestion of artifice in the pose and expression, a lack of the direct, unconscious sincerity which the same artist would have caught and conveyed in dealing with another sitter. So with even the greatest autobiographies. They are a mine of information which no biographer could overlook. They often afford the most startling and penetrating gleams of sudden veracity. Yet often also there is about them just the suggestion of artifice

239

and pose which belongs to the self-painting, a certain strain of unreality, quite different from the simple reflection of a soul which is living in the moment with no consciousness whatever of producing an effect on anyone else.

It is of the utmost interest to consider the variety of motives which induce thousands of people to commit their lives to writing in one form or another. Mrs. Anna Robeson Burr, in her extensive study of the Autobiography, has analyzed these motives, and the learned Professor Misch, in the only volume published of his exhaustive Teutonic survey of the same subject, also treats them at impressive length. There is the simple desire for record, for one's self, or for one's family, as when Darwin declares that he had no thought of publication. There is the possibility of a financial return, as with Moore, or Mrs. Oliphant. There is the pretext of edification, of making the world better by one's example, whether it is one to imitate or to avoid, as in the great religious model of Saint Augustine, and in many others since. There is the imitative instinct, the impulse to do what others have done and got glory by doing. There is the simple curiosity of getting deeper and deeper into one's own soul. Mrs. Burr, with the scientist's instinct for formula, unites with all these what she calls 'the autobiographical intention'; but I do not clearly understand what the mere name adds to a complication of the various motives suggested above.

BIOGRAPHY BY MIRROR

I think we shall somewhat clarify this matter of motive by remembering the two elementary instincts which form the basis of the biographical passion in general. There is first the intense interest in human life and the practical necessity for studying it. A very little of such study shows the immediate connection of our lives with the lives of others. If we are to know theirs, we must study our own, and *vice versa*. The great basis of social life and the stoutest tissue of conversation is the give-and-take based on the desire for such mutual knowledge. And the thoughtful and reflective soon come to see that a minute study of their own souls is the best preliminary to acquiring an intimate knowledge of others. Secondly, there is the still profounder instinct of getting out of ourselves into the lives and souls of others. The supreme manifestation of this instinct is the universal human desire for confession, to tell to someone, somewhere, somehow, the inmost secrets of our hearts, and in the hope of getting response, and understanding, and sympathy. The Catholic Church, with its perfect human tact, has seized upon this instinct and made it one of the most effective agents of domination and control. But the instinct works at all times, with all of us, in little things and great. We are impelled to confide in intimate converse with our friends. We are often betrayed into strange revelations with those who are almost unknown to us, revelations which make us shiver as we think them over afterwards.

BIOGRAPHY BY MIRROR

One of the most subtle and unveiling forms of confession is the epistolary, the habit of telling things by letter which we could not possibly utter by word of mouth.

It is odd that many persons who are extremely shy and reticent about discovering their secrets to any one individual, even by letter, suddenly drop their reticence, and go almost to an extreme of naked candor in making the general confessions of autobiography. The great autobiographies of the world have often come from people who, in their actual lives, have been peculiarly reserved and unapproachable, but who seem to have saved up the frankness of years to bestow it in ungarnered opulence upon the curious, or, alas, too often, the careless, ear of far-off posterity. Montaigne remarks how odd it is that, when a friend wants to know the inmost secrets of his heart, he has to recommend him to his bookseller. But the same thing has happened over and over, and always will. You shrink from intimate confidences with your own family. You hide your motives and your passions and your sufferings in dim corners, where the curious eye of your nearest friend cannot penetrate. Then you suddenly tear off the veil and fling the deepest tattered lining of the mystery out to be shaken and unraveled by the wind and sunshine of the open world. You pretend that you want absolute secrecy and silence. Yet at the same time, you are always speaking so that all the world may hear. In the words that Mrs. Burr quotes from

BIOGRAPHY BY MIRROR

Marie Bashkirtseff, you write 'as if no one in the world were to read it, yet with the purpose of being read.'

II

The peculiar feature of autobiography, and one too frequently and easily forgotten, is that it deals with the past and often with the remote past. This is especially noticeable when we compare it with letters and diaries, the supreme resource of the biographer. The letter-writer and the diarist are careless, often inaccurate, often misrepresent; but at least they are dealing with immediate matter of the moment, they take up the experience and set it down in the freshness of recent recollection and the quick veracity and vivacity of actual living. The autobiographer hunts and gropes in memory, picks up one thread and overlooks another, pieces them together often with his imagination, and produces a composite, which may have spiritual entirety and may not, but is perilously apt to mislead even the writer himself and much more those who read him.

The vast accumulation of autobiography appears in various more or less distinct types. There is the mainly external historical memoir, in which the subject simply makes himself a centre of observation to reflect the life and movement of the world about him, as in the mass of memoirs connected with the French Revolution and the Napoleonic period or the American Civil War. There is the personal story, in which the writer makes himself the main figure, but more for what he did than for what he was. There is the type in which the narrator has played a prominent public part, as Saint Augustine or Cellini, but is also a good deal interested in presenting the elements of his own personality as such. And there is the most introspective type of all, as Cardan or Rousseau, in which the interest of both author and reader is primarily centred, not upon events at all, but upon the various subjective experiences with which those events developed themselves in the writer's inner life.

But in all these types there is constantly this glimmering, shimmering mirror of memory, which the autobiographer has to consult and explore, before he can do his work at all, and the treachery of memory is unbelievable. Mrs. Burr energetically defends autobiography in general against the charge of unreliability. No doubt the autobiographer's intention and effort are usually sincere. He really aims and sets out to tell the truth. But he himself rarely appreciates how ready memory is to ensnare and entrap him, and it is only by the most close and careful criticism, if at all, that we can exercise satisfactory checks. 'Your mind is honest, but your memory a knave,' says Swift. It is a useful reminder in the employment of autobiography.

In most cases the farther back one probes into the past, the more unreliable does memory become.

BIOGRAPHY BY MIRROR

Now it is a peculiar tendency of all autobiographers to love to dwell upon the earlier portion of life. There is excellent justification for this. In the first place, remembered youth has charm for all of us, charm which in most cases probably did not so greatly affect the actual experiences, but which grows with distance and the sense of having lost what can never be renewed. Further, in writing about our lives we are anxious to tell what nobody else can. Plenty of those about us can give a narrative of our maturity, often more than we care for. But our early days are lost and we are eager to make the story complete, so far as it can be done. Lastly, the years of youth are the formative ones, those that really count in the building of character, and if our souls are to be explained at all, it must be in the influences that surrounded them when they were tender, easily moulded, when a month or a day would do more than ten years later on. Therefore, the writer of his own life dwells lovingly upon the first years, and these are just the years as to which his memory is likely to be least reliable, though he may not think so.

In nothing does the treachery of memory show more than in the tendency to report conversations. To recollect spoken words, even one's own, is extremely difficult, although only a short space of time may have elapsed since they were uttered. Unless speech is noted on the spot with stenographic accuracy, no reliance can be placed upon it. Yet autobiographers are perpetually asking us to accept long conversations when hours or months or years must have intervened between the uttering and the noting. The difference in the instinct of veracity in this respect is remarkable. One of the most conscientious of self-observers, Madame de Staal-Delaunay, records a parting interview with a lover whom she had deeply cherished. 'The interview was brief and not repeated,' she says; 'his mother was present; what was said has faded.' Fanny Burney, always genuine in intention, but an incurable romancer, would have given us three pages of elaborate talk.

This perpetual deception and peril of memory interweave themselves with certain other tendencies of autobiography, to produce a web of peculiar fragile tenuousness. There is, for instance, the extremely subtle and difficult element of self-praise. A man can hardly write a book about himself without giving himself some compliments, nor does he wish to. The disposition to exaggerate in this regard is born in all of us, at least to put our conduct in the most favorable light, if it is to be represented at all, and the obscuring, golden haze of memory is often of the greatest help to us, as we daily appreciate, whether we are writing formal autobiography or not.

Direct, whole-hearted self-praise is of course somewhat difficult to indulge in. Yet it is astonishing how often the autobiographer accomplishes it. This is Rousseau's final summary of his excellences: 'I was sure that, in spite of my faults and my weaknesses, in spite of my unwillingness to endure a rebuff of any sort, I should always be found just, kind, without gall, without hate, without jealousy, ready to recognize my own faults and still more ready to forget others', seeking all my felicity in kindly affections, and in all things carrying sincerity to imprudence, even to the point of incredible disinterestedness.' One could not say much more for one's best friend.

Generally praise is more indirect. One contrives somehow to let one's best friend say it. Again, it is possible to insinuate one's good points, and under the guise of modesty and shyness to imply things that might offend, if said right out. And there are endless devices for making the worse appear the better. 'It was my nature to take muleteers for honest people,' says Marmontel. In other words, by deploring one's excess of candor, or of good-nature, or of generosity, one can really get credit for virtues, while appearing to condemn one's self for faults.

It must be remembered that commending one's self is always a task of great difficulty and delicacy. If autobiographers, or you and I, were to say half the good we really like to think of ourselves, the world would mock us lavishly for vanity and conceit. But you can blame yourself without limit, and the world will pity and laud you for sincerity and honesty. Hence autobiographies are full of what appears to be the candid confession of faults. Franklin can make an elaborate list of his defects side by side with his virtues. Retz can weigh good and evil doing, from the moral point of view, and deliberately choose the latter, and 'get away with it,' with sympathetic commendation for his frankness.

Only, it must be appreciated that the faults on which autobiography dilates are apt to be those which the world is inclined to condone or to smile at. Chief among these are irregularities of sex, and Casanova can confess his large gayeties, secure that he will receive, if not open approval, at least a considerable amount of sympathy: 'To cultivate the pleasure of the senses was always my principal preoccupation; I have never had any other that was more important.' On the other hand, there are plenty of meannesses, sordid habits, contemptible, lurking motives, of which nobody is proud. Mark Twain tells us that he set out to record these fully, but found it quite impossible, and autobiographers in general are apt to behave very much like Mark. Yet Mrs. Burr's veracity of autobiographical intention has queer quirks of explosive directness, and Augustine and Rousseau and many others will unveil dusty and unclean corners with surprising nakedness, yet obviously often with the obscure desire to arouse pity, or sympathy, or understanding somewhere.

So it becomes clear enough that this elaborate complication of motives tending to distort and mislead, working with the natural betrayal of memory, amply suffices to make autobiography a

248

tangled web, as fascinating to unravel as it is difficult. And it may be taken for granted that the enthusiastic followers of Freud and the devotees of the 'new psychology' will see in it everywhere a maze of conflicts and complexes and hidden sex repressions, which may, or may not, account for a vast variety of autobiographical vagary.

III

To the writer and to the reader of biography there is less direct profit in merely external autobiography than in that which deals more with analysis of the writer's inner experience. Yet the external has often indirect biographical value of the highest order. There is a whole class of memoirs which gives indispensable light upon the life of a period and the historical events that took place in it. Such light is again subject to constant correction in allowance for the whims of memory, but it has often a personal flavor that more formal history can never give. For example, there is the vast group of memoirs dealing with Napoleonic France, and Ségur and Marbot bring Spain and Russia before us with a vividness that no later historian can rival. Or in the narratives of Grant and Sherman we have the American Civil War acted over again with intense vivacity of detail. And in the volumes of Lord Grey and Colonel House and a score of others we have the living record of the Great War, presented always from the personal angle, but all the more vivid on that account.

BIOGRAPHY BY MIRROR

There is not only the presentation of events, there is the study of characters, often affording the richest, if not the most reliable, material, for the use of the biographer. Dominating everything else in the Napoleonic group there is always the supremely fascinating figure of Napoleon himself. The *Memoirs* of Saint-Simon, interesting enough as a record of the writer, are far more so in their extraordinary picture of the men and women of his time, Louis XIV, Madame de Maintenon, the Regent Duke of Orléans, and a hundred others. There is no more wonderful portrait-gallery in the world. No doubt they are all drawn as Saint-Simon sees them, with a slant of passion, a slant of prejudice. But at least he helps us to see them for ourselves. In English history, Clarendon's collection is almost equally important, and no one who has read his characters of Buckingham or Cromwell can ever forget them, whether he agrees with them or not. A hundred years later, Lord Hervey makes George the Second and Queen Caroline and their Court stand out in the same way. Was a certain type of marital affection ever better touched off than in King George's cry to his dying wife, who implored him to marry again: '*Jamais! Jamais! J'aurai de maîtresses.*'

Also, there is the type of external biography which deals with the writer's own fortunes, but deals with him rather as acting than as reflecting. One of the earliest models of this type, and a model which has been imitated but never surpassed, is the *Commentaries* of Cæsar. In these we have apparently the dry, direct narrative of simple events. Yet somehow even here there is a cast of things that does not redound to the writer's discredit. History is full of similar personal records. Perhaps the one that comes nearest to us in America is that of General Grant, written with much of Cæsar's graphic power and with all of Cæsar's sincerity. Or, again, we have personal narratives of a more romantic and picturesque description, like the *Memoirs* of Alexandre Dumas, in which the quaint and whimsical vagaries of memory are almost taken for granted, and writer and reader both feel that they are wandering in a mist of delightful rosy uncertainty, with an extremely fragile hold upon fact, but a total result of decided and thoroughly human entertainment.

Another form of these autobiographies of action is the story of the great explorers, the travelers in the Polar regions, who have fully recorded their experience, like Dr. Kane, or more recently Shackleton, or those who have plunged into the centre of Africa, from Park to Roosevelt. The old witchery of such narratives was long ago gathered into the great collections of Hakluyt and Purchas. Nothing better illustrates the common humanity of biography than these stories of remote adventure. They might be supposed to be far away from the fat and indolent citizen — that is, you and me — sitting by his peaceful fireside, utterly unversed in perils by land or perils by water. Yet he has human courage in him, and human hope, and human endurance, above all, the profoundly human passion for success, and as he reads of these faraway struggles and sufferings and triumphs, he shares them with passionate imaginative ardor, and also revels with greater appreciation in all the comforts of home.

IV

But direct self-studies have generally more biographical interest and more human fascination than even the best external narratives. Naturally there is variation here also. Sometimes a writer will set out to portray himself, but, from lack of either ability or of real desire for truth, he will lose himself in a mass of superficial detail which merely wearies and confuses the reader. This is the case with the disappointing autobiography of Goethe, so acute and profound in his analysis of others, yet apparently unable or unwilling in his old age to apply this power to his own past.

But there are plenty of autobiographers who make an intense and passionate effort at veracity, though with varying success. Rousseau proclaims over and over his determination to tell the truth and nothing else. Gibbon begins his autobiography again and again, in the desire to make the most exact and complete presentation possible. Darwin declares that he writes of himself impersonally, as if he were looking back from the dead. Cardan, the great Renaissance physician and one of the first of careful analysts, announces that his predecessors have handed down unreliable narratives and not the sincere rendering that he attempts. Sometimes the autobiographer triumphantly asserts his honesty, would have the reader believe that he not only aims to tell the truth, but that he always tells it, as Gozzi proclaims, 'I would far rather frankly record facts to my discredit than bear the stings of conscience by suppressing what is true.' And Alfieri declares with equal assurance: 'I who was never known to forfeit my promise, here covenant with myself and my readers to free myself, as much as it is in the power of man to do, from the mist of passion and prejudice in the delineation of my own character.' And again, there is, more rarely, a keener self-critic, who, while making perhaps an even more conscientious effort at the facts, recognizes skeptically or sadly the extreme difficulty or even the impossibility of giving them. 'False glory and false modesty,' says Retz, 'are the two dangers which most of those who have written their own lives have not been able to escape.'

When one considers the direct result of these analyses, there is some disappointment, and one feels too often that, with all their keenness and all their concentration, these alert self-students are apt to be surprisingly deceived about themselves, though perhaps this is not strange when one considers the variety of elements of error that I have suggested earlier. But if the general effect of the self-portrayal is often misleading and erroneous, there is frequently an intense, an overpowering vigor and vividness of revelation in details and special incidents. How sudden and profound an insight do we get into Cellini's love and hate, or into the pitiful suffering of Rousseau. Franklin's sober mathematical summary of his vices and virtues may have its comic aspect, but it is extraordinarily illuminating for many besides himself. And Darwin's quiet dissection of his own intellectual powers is as subtle and as cool as if he were applying the same process in the animal world. And women are as capable of calm, detached self-observation as are men, though it may be somewhat less frequent with them. Take Madame de Staal-Delaunay's observations on the death of her father, and compare them with Pepys on similar occasions: 'I had never seen him, and I do not know if I believed I had one. I gave him a few tears, but really I do not now remember where they came from.'

But in autobiography an even greater interest attaches to what the writer reveals unintentionally than to his deliberate self-portrayal, and this is true of the greatest autobiographies, as of the least. We watch in Rousseau an elaborate and complete life and character-development along lines that the subject himself did not altogether contemplate, a tragic tumult of disaster bred out of elements of passion far different from those of which the painter endeavored to build his own likeness. So

with George Sand. Her narrative, taken in con-
junction with those of others, suggests subtle and
profound sub-conscious workings which make up a
total quite remote from the ideal picture she presents. Both are fascinating, but they are very different. Take a very recent autobiography, that of
Theodore Dreiser. The work is done with sincerity. It is profoundly attaching and convincing.
But the figure of the hero is one thing when you
survey him, as he does, in himself, and quite another when you go deeper and consider him as a
typical product of his age in comparison with other
ages. His utter lack of education and mental
training make him incapable of instituting this
comparison for himself, and it is in the revelation
of all that the comparison implies that the value of
his autobiography largely consists.

But, in general, the curious and intimate inter-
relation of self-knowledge and self-being and the
consequent startling failure of self-knowledge to
affect life and conduct tempt one constantly to
apply to all autobiography the admirable sentence
from *All's Well That Ends Well*: 'That this fellow
should know what he was and be what he is.'

v

It is obvious that the autobiographer is always
liable to the charge of extreme egotism. His object
is to talk about himself, his business is to talk about
himself, and the pronoun *I* is bound to be the chief
ornament of his pages from beginning to end.

BIOGRAPHY BY MIRROR

There is the indirect egotism which consists in considering one's self to be different from others, that is, being unique and exceptional, to be in consequence worthy of elaborate and minute discussion and description. Rousseau is the extreme instance of this, but it is always cropping up in more disguised forms, as in Mr. Dreiser's remark: 'I am of that peculiar disposition which will not let memories of old ties and old pleasures die easily. I suffer for things which might not give another a single ache or pain.' How many of us have thought the same thing at one time or another!

Or, there is the flaunting egotism of action, the *I* doing great deeds and saying great words, striding triumphantly along the rough life-path in spite of all obstacles, and elbowing the crowding fellow-shadows out of it with aggressive indifference. Sometimes the egotism is tempered by irony and humorous gayety, as in the *Memoirs* of Dumas. Sometimes it is sheerly passionate, direct, and forthright, as in Cellini, or in Lord Herbert of Cherbury. Sometimes it consists in the serene assurance that one is a favorite of Fortune and the constant subject of special attention from that capricious deity, as appears in the charming assertion of Goldoni: 'There was always something extraordinary in all my arrangements, and to say the truth, almost always to my advantage. I was born lucky, and whenever I have not been so, the fault has been entirely my own.' Again, the egotism may appear in an extreme susceptibility to the advancement and success of others. This is particularly evident in military narratives, because in the soldier's career so much depends upon rank and the steady progress from one grade to another. There is a pitiful display of such susceptibility in some of the memories of our own Civil War, as with Beauregard or Longstreet. On the other hand, it is hardly necessary to say that the autobiography of action does not always imply any such crude displaʲ of direct egotism. Even Cæsar is too proud for cheap boasting. Long before Cæsar we have in Xenophon's *Anabasis* a charming model of the narrative of great achievement with the self-narrating actor kept most modestly in the background. And again in the Civil War, the story of Grant is as simple and modest as that of Xenophon.

Also, there is the autobiography of humility, so to speak, the vast literature of religious confession, so elaborately studied by Mrs. Burr, in which the aim of the narrator is nominally to depreciate himself, to insist upon his own 'vileness,' to use the favorite word of one striking example, David Brainerd. Ever since Saint Augustine set the great example fifteen hundred years ago, sinners have been amplifying their wickedness, analyzing the dark and dirty corners of their hearts, throwing off every wrapping of reserve and shyness, the better to unveil the hidden depths of depravity. They have done this in part to encourage others, in part to show the power of grace and repentance and salvation, and also in part, it must be assumed, for the purpose of playing a considerable rôle in the world, in one way, if they cannot in another.

For here, too, however disguised the form, the *I* is still at work, and in too many cases of such confession we have still and only egotism masquerading as humility. No matter how you conceal it or obscure it, the *I* is the subject of autobiography: it always will be so, so long as autobiography is written at all. It is curious and charming to see how sensitive persons have sought for an obscuring veil. Thus, three hundred years ago, Lord Clarendon wrote his autobiography in the third person, not I, but Mr. Hyde did thus and thus. In our own generation, Henry Adams made the same attempt, and the reader gets Henry Adams, Henry Adams, instead of the capital I. It is doubtful if there is any material gain. The most curious of all efforts of the kind is that of the great French minister Sully, who resorted to the second person, and had his memoirs written by his secretary at his own dictation and addressed to himself as you, with an extraordinary effect of artificiality and remoteness, which rather increases the egotism than diminishes it. The truth is that all such attempts overlook the real and solid justification for all *I*-literature, which is, that the *I* is merely generic, and that the autobiographer, in writing about himself, is writing about you and me. If he were not, we would not listen to him for a moment.

BIOGRAPHY BY MIRROR

VI

Thus far, in internal autobiography, we have been considering the *I* and its relation to itself. It is almost equally interesting in its analysis of its relation to others. No life, not even the most solitary or introspective, is lived for itself alone. The main charm of Rousseau's *Confessions* lies undoubtedly in self-analysis, but how much there is besides in the variety and richness of the background, in the spirit and grace of the many purely incidental episodes, in the innumerable contrasted characters of men and women whom he is forced to introduce in describing himself.

There is the excitement, the stimulation, the varied emotion of all sorts, which a quick and eager spirit feels in the mere observing and contemplation of other lives. Sometimes, indeed, this contemplation is so incessant and so overwhelming that it leaves the individual too little power and inclination for living his own proper life. As Henry Adams expresses it, he himself, 'a nervous animal, made life a terror by seeing too much.' As Thoreau buried himself in the life of external nature, lost himself and seemed to become one with the trees and the flowers and the birds, so there are those whose existence seems to be merged in the existence of others, and to whom the study and consideration of other lives seems always to afford amusement and sometimes instruction and profit. An intense, a devouring, an insatiable curiosity makes a nature like Pepys' find in his contact with the great world an endless source of diversion. Saint-Simon notes and probes the doings of men, not only because he enters into them with passionate curiosity, but because he makes them an integral part of his own passions of love and hate. When his friends triumph, he riots in the joy of it. When his enemies are defeated, he bursts out into pæans of — of course righteous exultation. The hidden intensity of bitterness and ardor which he throws into these things shows in one brief touch, when he describes a colloquy with a shattered foe: 'The agony with which he felt his disaster blinded him to such an extent that he never saw that I was trying to make talk only to turn him into ridicule.' And Saint-Simon was a noble and even at times a humane spirit, but the intense passion of his humanity made him cruel as it is too apt to do with all of us.

For our human relations can never be confined to mere observing and impersonal study. We have to act and react and interact, and to let others act upon us, whether we will or no. All autobiography is full of the record, more or less distorted, of these contacts and reactions. Some human beings naturally seek such things, and some fly them. Some are drawn to their fellows, cannot be happy without them or apart from them. Some profess to fly them, and none can escape them altogether.

Sometimes the contact develops into the love of power and mastery. There seem to be those who are born to dominate others and who feel very little joy or interest in life except in doing so. This may degenerate into the extreme morbid forms which are often the delight of modern psychology. But in its more normal manifestations it is common to a great many men and women, to some who would be surprised if you attempted to make them aware of it. It is not only the conquerors and great kings who love to dominate: it is the merchant in his business office, it is the mother, or sometimes the son or the daughter, in the household. The instinct of mastery is as natural to certain creatures as is to others the opposite instinct, of rebellion, or of absolute independence.

And the correlative of mastery, especially when it is not achieved, is too often jealousy and mistrust. If you cannot conquer, you are disposed to undermine, and to assume that others are ready to undermine and betray you, and other autobiographies besides Rousseau's thus get full of doubt and envy and misjudgment and final despair.

Also, as some are born to revel in the sense of control and mastery, others are clinging and dependent, and this instinct again may go to abnormal extremes as the other often does. We have temperaments which naturally seek advice and guidance, turn to those whom they consider wiser and stronger for leadership and support in every step of their uncertain passage through the complicated journey of life. How curious it is to follow Rousseau's dependence upon Madame de Warens, upon the vulgar, violent, and arbitrary Thérèse, upon all the group of men and women who so greatly influenced him in Paris, the very depth and completeness and intensity of his abandon and confidence turning against him in the bitterness of his later suspicion and despair. Or you may have a nature like Alfieri's, haughty, self-sufficient, priding itself on its independence, its power to dispense with ordinary human relations and supports, yet in the end succumbing entirely to one engrossing affection, which becomes an essential and indispensable element of life.

The interesting question that arises in all this matter of frank internal autobiography is, how far have you the right, in confessing yourself, to confess others at the same time. Our lives are all so intricately bound up together that it is almost impossible to tell our own secrets without telling the secrets of others also.

In her elaborate and very charming history of her life, George Sand takes decided ground on this point of the confession of others. 'As regards the public,' she says, 'I do not allow myself the right to dispose of the past of all the persons whose existence has been associated with my own.' And she complains that Rousseau, in revealing his own experience in so much detail, was unavoidably revealing the experience of Madame de Warens also.

But, interesting as George Sand's narrative is, it is chiefly a story of absences, for this very reason; and, to understand her life and character, her own record has to be very largely supplemented by the records and the revelations of others. The truth is, that if you are to attempt veracious or serious autobiography at all, and there are serious doubts about the wisdom of doing so, you must deal with other lives besides your own. Rousseau, like George Sand herself, would have been quite incomprehensible without an inner glimpse, and from precisely his personal point of view, of all these other souls who influenced him. We cannot stand apart. We cannot portray ourselves without analyzing the intimate working of other lives upon ourselves. And in analyzing that working, we must analyze the lives to the best of our ability. The result will be complex, elusive, misleading, because all our analysis is so, of ourselves as well as of others. But one life is too close-knit a web ever to be extricated, or isolated, or to be presented single and alone. The best we can do is to keep veracity and justice of intention before us, in our dealings with others, as in our dealings with ourselves.

VII

In all the vast and sinuous course of autobiography through the ages, we can trace the presence of certain simple, universal elements of human life and human nature, elements which form biography in general, and emphasis upon these elements in the autobiographical connection will bring home to us once more the eternal and universal truth of human identity. The autobiographer may have lived a thousand years ago, or two thousand, his surroundings may have been altogether different from the smooth, serene, hypercivilized atmosphere in which we flourish. Yet still, under the superficial differences, we strike down to the common human impulses and motives which in one form or another agitate you and me, from the day we are born until the day we die.

There is love, the mighty passion of sex; and it sometimes seems as if autobiography were made of it, built of it. It is not only the more erotic autobiographies, like Rousseau's, or Casanova's; but if you turn to an apparently dry and mathematical temper and a purely logical brain, like John Stuart Mill, you find him breaking out into the strange and touching eulogy of the one woman who changed his career, in the complete spirit of the great typical love sentence of French comedy: *'en voilà encore une qui croit avoir inventé l'amour.'*

And the old common theme of money enters everywhere, the struggle to get it, the impossibility of keeping it, the astonishing ease with which it melts away. Augustine and Cardan and Rousseau, Goldoni and Dumas, to take great autobiographical types, all come into contact with money, with the *meum* and *tuum* somehow, and all suggest the same needs and difficulties in regard to it.

And ambition, the immense desire to succeed, to do something great in the world, and be recognized and honored as having done it, is so vital in autobiography that it might be considered the mere stuff of it, if love did not so ardently compete.

BIOGRAPHY BY MIRROR

There is Cellini, throwing every nerve into the effort to outdo his rivals, and describing with almost poetic passion the supreme triumph of the casting of the Perseus statue. There is Cardan, muffled in his strange Latin garment of the Renaissance, but murmuring through it words that might be spoken by many an ardent worker today: 'This one thing I know, that from my earliest childhood I burned with the inextinguishable desire of an immortal name.' And always there is the haughty disclaimer of ambition, carrying with it only the surer evidence of the underlying ardor, as in Chateaubriand's cry: 'All the mediocrities of the antechamber, of the offices, of the gazettes, of the cafés, have called me ambitious, and I have no ambition whatever.'

Nor are the weaknesses and defects wanting in autobiography, any more than the long efforts and the unconquerable desires. Physical weakness is a universal theme, developed, dilated upon, often conveniently pleaded as an excuse for the failure to accomplish the great things which would otherwise have infallibly been achieved. Meanness and spite and hate are visible enough, too visible, everywhere, sometimes elaborated and manifested with extraordinary candor and frankness, as in the furious quarrels of Cellini, sometimes veiled, even, it would seem, from the writer himself, yet obvious enough to the acute and careful observer, in the things that are omitted as well as in those that are set down.

BIOGRAPHY BY MIRROR

And always there are the ultimate questions and problems which confront and perplex and torment every human being from the earliest reflecting years, and which were just as present and just as insoluble to the autobiographer of a thousand years ago as they are to you and me today. There is death and there is the hereafter — if there is — and there is God, also with a large question-mark in so many autobiographies. The universality of these problems is one of the distinguishing marks of autobiography, as of biography in general. You may have the religious enthusiast. You may have an autobiographer like Mill, who confesses frankly: 'I am thus one of the very few examples in this country of one who has, not thrown off religious belief, but never had it.' In one type, as in the other, the problem is there, because we all have to die, we all have to meet death somehow, and God is the most apt term for the tremendous problems connected with that meeting. Somehow, somewhere, in beginning, middle, or end, of autobiography, or in all three, as in life, your life and mine, we are bound to meet with God.

VIII

In a sense it may be said that the quintessence of biography is to be found in the *Essays* of Montaigne. Mark Twain, when he decided to write the story of his own life, after long meditation, made up his mind that the way to do it was to throw aside all attempt at elaborate chronological narrative and simply to deal with each episode as it presented itself in memory with all the vividness of detail that the moment happened to suggest. It cannot be said that Mark's idea was very successful, as he carried it out, and it resulted in a rather disorderly hodge-podge that perplexes the reader instead of helping him. But Montaigne was far happier in an apparently haphazard procedure of much the same sort. The *Essays*, in their wide and wayward wandering, deal with almost every phase of the comic and tragic diversity of human life, and into all these phases the author contrives to infuse his own spirit, his own character, his own experience, not crudely or pretentiously, but in intimate contact with the experience of others, so as to bring out as perfectly as possible the large human identity, the unity of all lives with your life and my life. To use Montaigne's own words about his own method: 'Not to venture to speak freely about one's self shows something wrong in one's own heart... and he who judges widely and wisely plunges both hands into examples from his own life as well as from those of others.... I not only venture to speak of myself, but I speak of myself only: I thrust it in when I am discussing other things and slip away from my subject to do so.'

To Montaigne his own merits and excellences are matter of curious consideration, like those of others. He studies them with interest, he points them out with intimate detail and with entire candor. He is a lover of truth, he tells us, and the memory of a

267

lie, even excusable or necessary, pricks his conscience with enduring discomfort. He is most careful in the observance of his promise, carries it to the point of superstition. He hates cruelty, cannot endure to see or think of the infliction of pain, and though he is a keen huntsman, like so many in his generation, the suffering of captured game is always a distress to him.

Nor is he a bit more reticent about his defects and weaknesses, but strips the veil from them with a hand as steady and remorseless as it is untiring. Ignorance? His ignorance is unlimited, and he confesses it freely and at all times, the only salvation being that, as with Henry Adams, he doubts whether others know much more than he. Anger? He is grievously subject to it. In great crises he is prepared and exercises some sort of control, but the little unexpected irritations come upon him like a whirlwind, and he says and does things that he regrets. Physical needs, physical weakness, physical fear, all are known to him: why should he hesitate to show them freely, since, after all, they are just human nature, the common stuff and tissue of every human heart? Or, as he sums it up, 'I rarely repent, and my conscience is usually contented, not as being the conscience of an angel, or of a horse, but the conscience of a man.'

Through it all, what is most striking in Montaigne is the singular detachment with which he surveys the whole human scene — that is, the whole scene of himself — with pity, with tenderness, but also with a cool, abstract curiosity, as if he himself were simply another, and all of a thousand others were he. He feels wonder, he feels astonishment, he feels endless surprise and amusement, but he feels no more of these things in regard to himself than in regard to others: 'I have seen no monster or miracle in the world more remarkable than myself; time and custom use us to every oddity; but the more I frequent myself and know myself, the less I understand.' And with this detachment there is a serene naturalism, which has hardly been surpassed by any other autobiographer, or by anyone else. Even Shakespeare, whose naturalism seems equal to anyone's, makes the skeptic Jaques suggest a certain sadness in the natural process of growth and decay:

> And so from hour to hour we ripe and ripe,
> And then from hour to hour we rot and rot,
> And thereby hangs a tale.

The modern skeptic goes far beyond Jaques: 'Ripen! Ripen! We rot in some places, we harden in others: we never ripen!' To Montaigne the process, just because it is natural, is acceptable, and is even not without a certain tranquil beauty of perfect fulfillment: 'The course of my bodily life has brought about each thing in its orderly season: I have seen the plant, and the flowers, and the fruit; now I see the withering of it, happily, because naturally.'

The lady in the lively modern comedy has a

BIOGRAPHY BY MIRROR

quick and vivid figure for revivals and re-surveyals of the buried past like those of Montaigne. 'Do you ever wish you were different?' she says. 'Probably you don't. I don't always. But there are times — when one would like to make one's self over, like an old frock. You've done that? Rip out all the seams, and turn this front breadth, where you got the bad spot when Mrs. Jones spilt the ice cream on you, put in new if you could only match it, but you can't, and get new passementerie, for the front of the waist, and bring the sleeves into style — and then, after all, it's an old frock still, and everybody knows it, and the worst of it is, it isn't a frock at all, it's your soul, and you can never, never get another.' But Montaigne has not even the touch of humorous despair which breathes through this gay summary. His method of treating his past, his life, himself, Michel de Montaigne, is simply that of one who goes to a wardrobe and takes down an old garment and brushes it caressingly, shaking out a moth or a crumb here, noting the creases and the patches, and distilling from it all a strange, sweet relish of reminiscence, which touches good and evil both with a clinging charm of melancholy grace.

THE END

APPENDIX

APPENDIX

COMPLETE REFERENCE LIST

As Gamaliel Bradford's portraits, or psychographs, as he called them, of great characters, past and present, ran to well over a hundred, the demand has arisen for the complete list, showing in what volume each may be found. It is hoped that the following list, alphabetically arranged, of all the portraits will be helpful both to old readers who may wish to renew acquaintance with some favorite essay, and to new ones who wish the aid of his incomparable analysis in the study of some elusive personality.

Adams, Abigail: *Portraits of American Women*, 1919
Adams, Henry: *American Portraits*, 1922
Alcott, Louisa May: *Portraits of American Women*, 1919
Arnold, Benedict: *Damaged Souls*, 1923
Arnold, Mrs. Benedict: *Wives*, 1925
Austen, Jane: *Portraits of Women*, 1916

Barnum, P. T.: *Damaged Souls*, 1923
Beauregard, P. G.: *Confederate Portraits*, 1914
Benjamin, Judah P.: *Confederate Portraits*, 1914
Bernhardt, Sarah: *Daughters of Eve*, 1930
Blaine, James Gillespie: *American Portraits*, 1922
Blaine, Mrs. James G.: *Wives*, 1925
Booth, Edwin: *As God Made Them*, 1929
Borgia, Cæsar: *Saints and Sinners*, 1932
Bowles, Samuel: *Union Portraits*, 1916
Brown, John: *Damaged Souls*, 1923
Burr, Aaron: *Damaged Souls*, 1923
Burr, Theodosia: *Wives*, 1925
Burton, Robert: *A Naturalist of Souls*, 1926
Butler, Benjamin Franklin: *Damaged Souls*, 1923

APPENDIX

Butler, Mrs. Benjamin F.: *Wives*, 1925
Byron, George Gordon, Lord: *Saints and Sinners*, 1932

Calhoun, John Caldwell: *As God Made Them*, 1929
Casanova, Giacomo: *Saints and Sinners*, 1932
Catherine the Great: *Daughters of Eve*, 1930
Child, Francis James: *As God Made Them*, 1929
Choiseul, Mme. de: *Portraits of Women*, 1916
Clarendon, Earl of (Edward Hyde): *A Naturalist of Souls*, 1926
Clay, Henry: *As God Made Them*, 1929
Cleveland, Grover: *American Portraits*, 1922
Coolidge, Calvin: *The Quick and the Dead*, 1931
Cowper, William: *Bare Souls*, 1924
Cushman, Charlotte: *Biography and the Human Heart*, 1932

D'Arblay, Mme.: *Portraits of Women*, 1916
Darwin, Charles: *Darwin*, 1926
Davis, Mrs. Jefferson: *Wives*, 1925
Deffand, Mme. du: *Portraits of Women*, 1916
Dickinson, Emily: *Portraits of American Women*, 1919
Donne, John: *A Naturalist of Souls*, 1926
Dumas, Alexandre: *A Naturalist of Souls*, 1926

Edison, Thomas Alva: *The Quick and the Dead*, 1931

Fénelon: *Saints and Sinners*, 1932
Fitzgerald, Edward: *Bare Souls*, 1924
Flaubert, Gustave: *Bare Souls*, 1924
Ford, Henry: *The Quick and the Dead*, 1931
Francis, St., of Assisi: *Saints and Sinners*, 1932
Francis, St., of Sales: *A Naturalist of Souls*, 1926

Gray, Asa: *As God Made Them*, 1929
Gray, Thomas: *Bare Souls*, 1924
Greeley, Horace: *As God Made Them*, 1929
Guérin, Eugénie de: *Portraits of Women*, 1916
Guyon, Mme.: *Daughters of Eve*, 1930

APPENDIX

Holland, Elizabeth, Lady: *Portraits of Women*, 1916
Hooker, Joseph: *Union Portraits*, 1916
Hunt, William Morris: *Biography and the Human Heart*, 1932

James, Henry: *American Portraits*, 1922
Jefferson, Joseph: *American Portraits*, 1922
Johnston, J. E.: *Confederate Portraits*, 1914
Jones, John Beauchamp: *Biography and the Human Heart*, 1932

Keats, John: *Bare Souls*, 1924
Kempis, Thomas à: *Saints and Sinners*, 1932

Lamb, Charles: *Bare Souls*, 1924
Lanier, Sidney: *American Portraits*, 1922
Lee, Robert E.: *Lee the American*, 1912
Lemaître, Jules: *A Naturalist of Souls*, 1926
Lenclos, Ninon de: *Daughters of Eve*, 1930
Lenin, Nikolai: *The Quick and the Dead*, 1931
Leopardi, Giacomo: *A Naturalist of Souls*, 1926
Lespinasse, Mlle.: *Daughters of Eve*, 1930
Lincoln, Mrs. Abraham: *Wives*, 1925
Longfellow, Henry Wadsworth: *Biography and the Human Heart*, 1932
Longstreet, James: *Confederate Portraits*, 1914
Lyon, Mary: *Portraits of American Women*, 1919

McClellan, George Brinton: *Union Portraits*, 1916
Madison, Mrs. James: *Wives*, 1925
Maintenon, Mme. de: *Daughters of Eve*, 1930
Meade, George Gordon: *Union Portraits*, 1916
Montagu, Lady Mary Wortley: *Portraits of Women*, 1916
Moody, Dwight L.: *D. L. Moody: A Worker in Souls*, 1927
Mussolini, Benito: *The Quick and the Dead*, 1931

Ossoli, Margaret Fuller: *Portraits of American Women*, 1919
Ovid: *A Naturalist of Souls*, 1926

Paine, Thomas: *Damaged Souls*, 1923
Pater, Walter: *A Naturalist of Souls*, 1926

275

APPENDIX

Pepys, Samuel: *The Soul of Samuel Pepys*, 1924
Pepys, Mrs. Samuel: *Portraits of Women*, 1916
Pliny the Younger: *A Naturalist of Souls*, 1926

Randolph, John, of Roanoke: *Damaged Souls*, 1923
Ripley, Sarah Alden: *Portraits of American Women*, 1919
Roosevelt, Theodore: *The Quick and the Dead*, 1931

Sand, George (Amandine Aurore Lucie Dupin): *Daughters of Eve*, 1930
Semmes, Raphael: *Confederate Portraits*, 1914
Sévigné, Mme. de: *Portraits of Women*, 1916
Seward, William Henry: *Union Portraits*, 1916
Sherman, William Tecumseh: *Union Portraits*, 1916
Stanton, Edwin McMasters: *Union Portraits*, 1916
Stephens, Alexander H.: *Confederate Portraits*, 1914
Stowe, Harriet Beecher: *Portraits of American Women*, 1919
Stuart, J. E. B.: *Confederate Portraits*, 1914
Sumner, Charles: *Union Portraits*, 1916

Talleyrand-Périgord, Charles Maurice de: *Saints and Sinners*, 1932
Thomas, George Henry: *Union Portraits*, 1916
Toombs, Robert: *Confederate Portraits*, 1914
Trollope, Anthony: *A Naturalist of Souls*, 1926
Twain, Mark (Samuel Langhorne Clemens): *American Portraits*, 1922

Very, Jones: *Biography and the Human Heart*, 1932
Voltaire: *Bare Souls*, 1924

Walpole, Horace: *Bare Souls*, 1924; *Biography and the Human Heart*, 1932
Webster, Daniel: *As God Made Them*, 1929
Whistler, James McNeil: *American Portraits*, 1922
Whitman, Walt: *Biography and the Human Heart*, 1932
Willard, Frances Elizabeth: *Portraits of American Women*, 1919
Wilson, Woodrow: *The Quick and the Dead*, 1931

INDEX

INDEX

Adams, Henry, quoted, 4, 31, 259; his Autobiography, 258, 268
Adams, John, and Jefferson, 24
Adams, John Quincy, his disappointments, 16; his *Diary*, 20
Alfieri, Vittorio, 262; quoted, 253
Allston, Washington, 138
Ambition, a universal element of biography, 10–13, 264, 265
Amiel, Henri Frédéric, 18, 21, 92
Andrews, William P., editor of Very's poems, 187, 188, 192, 198
Autobiography, artifice of, 239; motives for, 240; candor of, 242; deals with the past, 243; types of, 243, 244, 250–52, 255; tendencies of, 245–49; material of, of value to biographer, 249, 250; as to veracity of, 252–55; egotism in, 255–58; the *I* in relation to others in, 259–63; universal elements of, 263–66

Barbellion, W. N. P., 18
Bashkirtseff, Marie, 243
Beauregard, P. G. T., 257
Benjamin, Judah P., Jones on, 156, 182
Biographer, the art of the, 6, 7
Biography, the eternal interest in, 3–5; origin of, 5; human identity as basis of, 8–22, 27, 30, 263–66; human difference as an element of, 23–26; iconoclastic, 27, 28; critical, 28; the exemplary, 29; its possibilities in education, 30–33; instincts at bottom of, 241; autobiographical matter of value to, 249; the quintessence of, 266–70
Blaine, James G., 18, 78
Brainerd, David, 257
Brown, John, 139
Buckingham, Duke of, 250
Burke, Edmund, Walpole on, 230

Burney, Fanny, 246
Burr, Aaron, his *Diary*, 18
Burr, Anna Robeson, her study of the Autobiography, 240, 242, 244, 248, 257
Butler, Benjamin F., 18
Butler, Sarah, 9
Byron, Lord, 205

Cæsar, Julius, his *Commentaries*, 252, 257
Camus, Bishop of Bellay, his Life of Saint Francis of Sales, 74
Cardan, G., 244, 252, 264, 265
Carlyle, Thomas, 50
Carlyle, Mrs. Thomas, 110, 116
Casanova, Giovanni J., 18, 248, 264
Cellini, Benvenuto, 19, 244, 254, 256, 265
Chateaubriand, François René, quoted, 165
Chatham, William Pitt, Earl of, Walpole on, 227
Chatterton, Thomas, and Walpole, 230
Chesnut, Mary Boykin, her *Diary*, 165
Choiseul, Madame de, 232
Cicero, his ambition, 11
Civil War, American, conditions in Richmond during, 160–68, 176–79; dramatic character of, 168, 169, 176, 184; confidence of Southerners, 174–76; bitterness of Southerners toward Yankees, 178, 179
Clarendon, Edward Hyde, Earl of, 250, 258
Clement, Clara Erskine, 119
Coke, Lady Mary, Walpole's letters to, 216, 222
Coleridge, Samuel T., 61
Cooper, Samuel, 181
Cromwell, Oliver, 25, 250

279

INDEX

Cushman, Charlotte, her ambition, 12, 100, 101; chronology of her life, 96; imagination and conscience in, 97, 117; her career, 97, 98; her passion for her art, 98, 99, 105, 106; her acting, 101; her glory, 101–03; her failures, 103–05; her various decisions to retire, 104; her enjoyment of poetry and music, 105, 106; her interest in social life, 106, 107; as a talker, 107; her social manner, 108; her devotion to members of family, 109; her love-experience, 109, 110; her women-friends, 110, 111; her prejudices, 111, 112; her appearance, 113; her habit of industry, 113; her virile character, 113, 114; her aptitude for business and desire of money, 114, 115; her desire to dominate, 115; her intelligence, 116; her moral qualities, 117–23; her religion, 121, 122; her self-control, 123, 124

Dante Alighieri, Longfellow's translation of, 60
Darwin, Charles, 17, 26; his Autobiography, 240, 252, 254
Daudet, Alphonse, quoted, 15
Davis, Jefferson, Jones on, 173, 174, 182, 183
Death, universal element in biography, 20, 21, 266
Deffand, Madame du, Walpole's letters to, 216; her passion for Walpole, 222, 224; and Madame de Choiseul, 232; life a bore to, 234
Dickinson, Emily, 121, 140
Doyle, Peter, 87
Dreiser, Theodore, quoted, 22; his Autobiography, 255, 256
Dumas, Alexandre, 61, 264; *Memoirs* of, 251, 256
Duyckink brothers, Whitman's description of, 78

Edison, Thomas A., 16
Egotism, in autobiography, 255–58

Emerson, Ralph Waldo, on Longfellow, 37; to Whitman, 65; comment of Whitman on, 77; Whitman's use of letter of, for advertising purposes, 82; painting of, 134; on Very's poetry, 187, 203; his influence of style on Very's writing, 190, 192; Very compared with, 201, 202
Epic Poetry, Very's essay on, 189–91
Epictetus, 202
Espinasse, Mlle. de L', 10

Fear, element in biography, 21
Fields, J. T., Hunt to, 136
Fields, Mrs. J. T., letter of Charlotte Cushman to, 102; quoted on Charlotte Cushman, 108, 112; on Hunt, 136
Forrest, Edwin, and Charlotte Cushman, 119
Franklin, Benjamin, 247, 254
Frederick the Great, his ambition, 11; Rousseau on, 27
Fuller, Margaret, 51

Gibbon, Edmund, his Autobiography, 252
God, in biography, 21, 22, 266
Goethe, Johann Wolfgang von, 16; his Autobiography, 252
Goldoni, Carlo, 264; quoted, 256
Goncourts, the, 21
Gough, John B., 18
Gozzi, Carlo, quoted, 253
Grant, Gen. U.S., 20, 25; in *Memoirs*, 251
Gray, Thomas, on possession of money, 14; his dejection, 15; and Walpole, 230
Greville, quoted, 4
Guérin, Maurice de, 198
Gurowski, Count, 41

Hakluyt, Richard, 251
Hate, in biography, 18, 19
Haydon, Benjamin Robert, his *Diary*, 13, 18

INDEX

Health, physical, 16, 17; moral, 17
Heine, Heinrich, quoted, 19
Herbert, George, 201
Herbert of Cherbury, Lord, 256
Heroes, 27
Hervey, Lord, 250
Holmes, Oliver Wendell, 134
Howells, William Dean, on Longfellow, 37, 57, 58
Hunt, William Morris, chronology of his life, 126; his career, 127, 128; his painting, 128; as a painter, 129–37; his shrewdness in business matters, 138; as reader and student, 138, 139; his religion, 139, 140; his passion for beauty, 140, 146, 151, 152; his enjoyment of music, 140; his fondness for horses, 141; his human sympathy, 141–43; his appearance, 143, 144; his charm, 143–46; his social freaks and fancies, 144; as teacher, 146–49; his *Talks on Art*, 148; his attitude toward criticism, 149, 150; his influence, 149–51

Jackson, Thomas Jonathan, Jones on, 173
James, Henry, Whitman on, 75; on Hunt, 141, 144
Jefferson, Joseph, on Charlotte Cushman, 107; on Forrest, 119
Jefferson, Thomas, and John Adams, 24
Jesse, John Heneage, his *George Selwyn and his Contemporaries*, 232
Johnson, Dr. Samuel, 19; his dread of death, 21; Walpole on, 231
Johnston, Gen. Albert Sidney, quoted, 131
Johnston, Gen. Joseph E., 87
Jones, John Beauchamp, chronology of his life, 154; his career, 155, 158–60; his diary, 155–59; his novels, 158, 159; in domestic duties, 160, 161; conditions at Richmond during the Civil War as depicted in his *Diary*, 160–68, 176–79; his intel-

lectual power, 167–70; his Diary compared to chorus of Greek Tragedy, 169, 174, 184; his political views, 170–72; his practical suggestions, 172, 173; his comment on men, 173, 174, 179–83; his confidence in triumph of Southern cause, 174, 175

Kane, Dr. Elisha Kent, 251
Keats, John, 9, 17, 61, 205, 208

Lanier, Sidney, 17, 68
Lee, Gen. Robert E., 20, 25; Jones on, 173, 181
Lee, Sir Sidney, 5, 29
Liberal education, 30, 31
Lincoln, Abraham, 175; on Whitman, 85
Lodge, Mr., on Charlotte Cushman, 114
Longfellow, Henry Wadsworth, chronology of his life, 36; his goodness, 37, 38; his modesty, 38, 39; his conscience, 40; his understanding and love of men, 40–42; his tenderness for family, 42; his sympathy with children, 42; his genius for friendship, 42–44; attraction of society for, 44; his sources of happiness, 45–47; his optimism, 47, 48; vexations of, 48–52; death of first wife, 53; his capacity for emotion, 53–56; as to his depth of thought, 56; his religion, 56; his distinction of character, 57; distinction lacking in his writings, 58–61; his translation of Dante, 60; the secret of his literary success, 61, 62; the poet of democracy, 71
Longstreet, James, 257
Lope de Vega, 61
Louis XIV, 250
Love, a universal element of biography, 8–10, 264
Lowell, James Russell, on Longfellow, 37, 58

Macaulay, Thomas B., and Very,

281

INDEX

191 *n.*; on Walpole, 221, 225, 227, 233

Macready, Henry, 99

Maintenon, Madame de, 250

Mallory, Stephen Russell, Jones on, 182

Marmontel, Jean François, quoted, 247

Memminger, Christopher Gustavus, Jones on, 182

Memoirs, 243, 249–51, 258

Mill, John Stuart, and Rousseau, 24; his Autobiography, 264, 266

Milton, John, and Shakespeare, 194, 195

Misch, Prof. Georg, his study of the Autobiography, 240

Money, element of, in biography, 13, 14, 264

Montagu, George, letters of Walpole to, 219, 222, 224

Montagu, Lady Mary, Walpole on, 231

Montaigne, Michel de, *Essays* of, 242, 266–70

Napoleon, 16, 25, 250

Newcastle, Duke of, Walpole on, 228

Northrop, Confederate commissary general, 180

Oliphant, Mrs., 240

Orléans, Regent Duke of, 250

Park, Mungo, 251

Pepys, Samuel, his *Diary*, 9, 13, 18, 155; compared with Longfellow, 48; Jones compared with, 156–58; compared with Walpole, 226; curiosity of, 260

Perry, Prof. Bliss, 75, 82

Pitt, Anne, Walpole's letters to, 216

Plutarch, 29

Poe, Edgar Allan, 51

Presidents, American, 26

Purchas, Samuel, 251

Rachel, Mme., actress, 104

Randolph, Thomas Jefferson, Jones on, 182

Retz, Jean François de, 248, 253

Richardson, Samuel, Walpole on *Clarissa Harlowe*, 231

Richmond, Virginia, in the Civil War, 160–68, 176–79

Roosevelt, Theodore, 24; his African narrative, 251

Rousseau, Jean Jacques, 18, 27, 248; his *Confessions*, 23, 244, 246, 252, 254, 256, 259, 261–64

Ruskin, John, quoted, 44

Saint Augustine, the *Confessions*, 18, 240, 244, 248, 257, 264

Saint-Simon, Louis de Rouvroy, Duke de, compared with Walpole, 226, 232; *Memoirs* of, 250, 260

Sainte-Beuve, Charles Augustin, 7, 8, 198, 199

Sand, George, 10, 255, 262, 263

Schwob, Marcel, quoted, 6

Scott, Sir Walter, 17

Seddon, James A., Jones on, 156, 170, 182

Selwyn, George, and Gilly Williams, 232

Sévigné, Madame de, 219, 220

Sex, a universal element of biography, 18, 264

Shackleton, Sir Ernest Henry, 251

Shakespeare, William, his 'book education,' 68; his humor, 79; rhythms of, 106; Very's essay on, 191–97; quoted, 269

Shelley, P. B., 61, 205

Sherman, Whitman's portrayal of, 75

Smith, G. W., 181

Southern Confederacy, dramatic character of, 168, 169, 176, 184

Spenser, Edmund, 209, 211

Staal-Delaunay, Madame de, 246, 254

Stebbins, Emma, quoted on Charlotte Cushman, 108, 115, 116

Sterne, Laurence, Walpole on his *Tristram Shandy*, 231

282

INDEX

Stevenson, Robert Louis, distinction in his verse, 59
Stillman, W. J., as critic of Charlotte Cushman, 108, 111, 112, 115, 117, 118
Story, William Wetmore, on Charlotte Cushman's singing, 106
Sully, Maximilien de Béthune, 258
Sumner, Charles, 44, 52
Supermen, 27
Swift, Jonathan, quoted, 244
Swinburne, Algernon Charles, Whitman's summary of, 75

Tennyson, Alfred, 105
Thayer, William R., 5
Thomas à Kempis, *Imitation of Christ*, 9, 201
Thoreau, Henry David, 259
Toombs, Robert, Jones on, 173
Townshend, Charles, Walpole on, 227, 228
Toynbee, Mrs. Paget, editor of Walpole's letters, 215-17, 227, 230
Traubel, Horace, his picture of Whitman, 73, 74, 82, 83
Twain, Mark, 248, 266, 267

Vernon, Prof. Ambrose White, his effort to build up academic department of Biography, 32
Very, Jones, chronology of his life, 186; career, 187, 188; editions of his writings, 188; his prose, 189-97; his lack of taste, 197, 209; his poetry, 198-212; his attitude toward Christ, God, and Nature, 198-208, 211, 212
Vocational training, 31
Voltaire, François de, his ambition, 11; quoted, 13, 31, 49; correspondence of, 215; Walpole on, 231

Walpole, Horace, chronology of his life, 214; his correspondence, 215-20; his career, 218, 219; his literary work, 218; his character, 221-24; his politics, 221, 225; his affections,

224; opposed to war and unnecessary cruelty, 225, 226; and George the Third, 226; his word-portraits, 227-29; his literary gossip and criticism, 229-31; his picture of social world, 231-35
Walpole, Sir Robert, 218, 224
Watts, Isaac, 201
Webster, Daniel, death of, 7; his ambition, 12; J. Q. Adams's comment on, 20
Weems, Mason Locke, his *Life of Washington*, 29
Welles, Gideon, 157
Whitman, Sarah W., quoted on Hunt, 129
Whitman, Walt, chronology of his life, 64; his relation to his own work, 65-73; Traubel's picture of, 73, 74; his hatred of partisanship, 74; his shrewdness, 75; his tenderness, 75, 76; his political optimism, 76, 77, 91, 92; his faith in humanity, 77; his spiritual contentment, 78; his humor, 78, 79; was a sun-lover, 79; his garrulity, 79; his meekness, 80; his egotism, 80, 82, 89; his book, 81; was widely praised, 81; his lack of delicacy, 82; his violent temper, 82; his obstinate persistence, 83; his physical vigor, 83, 84; his presence, 84, 85; his mental sanity, 85; his freedom of living, 85, 86; letters to his mother, 86; his male friendships, 87; his work in Washington hospitals, 87-89; his *Leaves of Grass*, 89-93; and God, 92, 93
Williams, Gilly, and George Selwyn, 232
Wilson, Woodrow, 24
Winder, Gen. John H., 180
Winter, William, on Charlotte Cushman, 118
Wordsworth, William, 205, 209

Xenophon, the *Anabasis*, 257

Zola, Émile, 68

283